PENGUIN BOOK

Bird

BIRDS OF SELBORNE

Gilbert White

English Journeys

PENGUIN BOOKS

Published by the Penguin Group
Penguin Books Ltd, 80 Strand, London WC2R ORL, England
Penguin Group (USA) Inc., 375 Hudson Street, New York, New York 10014, USA
Penguin Group (Canada), 90 Eglinton Avenue East, Suite 700, Toronto, Ontario, Canada M4P 2Y3
(a division of Pearson Penguin Canada Inc.)
Penguin Ireland, 25 St Stephen's Green, Dublin 2, Ireland
(a division of Penguin Books Ltd)
Penguin Group (Australia), 250 Camberwell Road, Camberwell, Victoria 3124, Australia
(a division of Pearson Australia Group Pty Ltd)
Penguin Books India Pvt Ltd, 11 Community Centre, Panchsheel Park, New Delhi – 110 017, India
Penguin Group (NZ), 67 Apollo Drive, Rosedale, North Shore 0632, New Zealand
(a division of Pearson New Zealand Ltd)
Penguin Books (South Africa) (Pty) Ltd, 24 Sturdee Avenue, Rosebank, Johannesburg 2196, South Africa

Penguin Books Ltd, Registered Offices: 80 Strand, London WC2R ORL, England

www.penguin.com

These extracts taken from *The Natural History of Selborne*, first published 1788–9
Published in Penguin Books 2009
1

All rights reserved

Set by Rowland Phototypesetting Ltd, Bury St Edmunds, Suffolk
Printed in England by Clays Ltd, St Ives plc

978-0-141-19093-8

www.greenpenguin.co.uk

Penguin Books is committed to a sustainable future
for our business, our readers and our planet.
The book in your hands is made from paper
certified by the Forest Stewardship Council.

A Note on the Text

The following text are letters taken from Gilbert White's *The Natural History of Selborne* (1788). As indicated, the first half of the letters were written to the zoologist, Thomas Pennant, and the second half to explorer and naturalist, Daines Barrington. The extracted letters in this edition reflect White's correspondences during the period 1767 to 1787.

Letters to Thomas Pennant

The parish of Selborne lies in the extreme eastern corner of the county of Hampshire, bordering on the county of Sussex, and not far from the county of Surrey; is about fifty miles south-west of London, in latitude 51, and near midway between the towns of Alton and Petersfield. Being very large and extensive, it abuts on twelve parishes, two of which are in Sussex, viz., Trotton and Rogate. If you begin from the south and proceed westward, the adjacent parishes are Emshot, Newton Valance, Faringdon, Harteley Mauduit, Great Ward le ham, Kingsley, Hedleigh, Bramshot, Trotton, Rogate, Lysse, and Greatham. The soils of this district are almost as various and diversified as the views and aspects. The high part to the south-west consists of a vast hill of chalk, rising three hundred feet above the village; and is divided into a sheep down, the high wood, and a long hanging wood called the Hanger. The covert of this eminence is altogether beech, the most lovely of all forest trees, whether we consider its smooth rind or bark, its glossy foliage, or graceful pendulous boughs. The down, or sheep-walk, is a pleasing park-like spot, of about one mile by half that space, jutting out on the verge of the hill-country, where it begins to break down into the plains, and commanding a very engaging view, being an assemblage of hill, dale, wood-lands, heath, and water.

The prospect is bounded to the south-east and east by the vast range of mountains called the Sussex-downs, by Guild-down near Guildford, and by the Downs round Dorking, and Ryegate in Surrey, to the north-east, which altogether, with the country beyond Alton and Farnham, form a noble and extensive outline.

At the foot of this hill, one stage or step from the uplands, lies the village, which consists of one single straggling street, three-quarters of a mile in length, in a sheltered vale, and running parallel with the Hanger. The houses are divided from the hill by a vein of stiff clay (good wheat-land), yet stand on a rock of white stone, little in appearance removed from chalk; but seems so far from being calcareous, that it endures extreme heat. Yet that the freestone still preserves somewhat that is analogous to chalk, is plain from the beeches which descend as low as those rocks extend, and no farther, and thrive as well on them, where the ground is steep, as on the chalks.

The cart-way of the village divides, in a remarkable manner, two very incongruous soils. To the south-west is a rank-clay, that requires the labour of years to render it mellow; while the gardens to the north-east, and small enclosures behind, consist of a warm, forward, crumbling mould, called *black malm*, which seems highly saturated with vegetable and animal manure; and these may perhaps have been the original site of the town; while the wood and coverts might extend down to the opposite bank.

At each end of the village, which runs from south-east to north-west, arises a small rivulet: that at the north-west end frequently fails; but the other is a fine perennial spring, little influenced by drought or wet seasons, called Well-head. This breaks out of some high grounds joining to Nore Hill, a noble chalk promontory, remarkable for sending forth two streams into two different seas. The one to the south becomes a branch of the Arun, running to Arundel, and so falling into the British Channel: the other to the north. The Selborne stream makes one branch of the Wey; and meeting the Black-down stream at Hedleigh, and the Alton and Farnham stream at Tilford-bridge, swells into a considerable river, navigable at Godalming from whence it passes to Guildford, and so into the Thames at Weybridge; and thus at the Nore into the German Ocean.

Our wells, at an average, run to about sixty-three feet, and when sunk to that depth seldom fail; but produce a fine limpid water, soft to the taste, and much commended by those who drink the pure element, but which does not lather well with soap.

To the north-west, north and east of the village, is a range of fair enclosures, consisting of what is called a *white malm*, a sort of rotten or rubble stone, which, when turned up to the frost and rain, moulders to pieces, and becomes manure to itself.

Still on to the north-east, and a step lower, is a kind of white land, neither chalk nor clay, neither fit for pasture nor for the plough, yet kindly for hops, which root deep into the freestone, and have their poles and wood for charcoal growing just at hand. This white soil produces the brightest hops.

As the parish still inclines down towards Wolmer-forest, at the juncture of the clays and sand the soil becomes a wet, sandy loam, remarkable for timber, and infamous for roads. The oaks of Temple and Blackmoor stand high in the estimation of purveyors and have furnished much naval timber; while the trees on the freestone grow large, but are what workmen call *shakey*, and so brittle as often to fall to pieces in sawing. Beyond the sandy loam the soil becomes an hungry lean sand, till it mingles with the forest; and will produce little without the assistance of lime and turnips.

*   *   *

In the court of Norton-farmhouse, a manor farm to the north-west of the village, on the white malms, stood within these twenty years a broad-leaved elm, or wych hazel, *ulmus folio latissimo scabro* of Ray, which, though it had lost a considerable leading bough in the great storm in the year 1703, equal to a moderate tree, yet, when felled, contained eight loads of timber; and, being too bulky for a carriage, was sawn off at seven feet above the butt, where it measured near eight feet in the diameter. This elm I mention to show to what a bulk planted elms may attain; as this tree must certainly have been such from its situation.

In the centre of the village, and near the church, is a square piece of ground surrounded by houses, and vulgarly called the Plestor. In the midst of this spot stood, in old times, a vast oak, with a short squat body, and huge horizontal arms extending almost to the extremity of the area. This venerable tree, surrounded with stone steps, and seats above them, was the delight of old and young, and a place of much resort in summer evenings;

where the former sat in grave debate, while the latter frolicked and danced before them. Long might it have stood, had not the amazing tempest in 1703 overturned it at once, to the infinite regret of the inhabitants, and the vicar, who bestowed several pounds in setting it in its place again; but all his care could not avail; the tree sprouted for a time, then withered and died. This oak I mention to show to what a bulk planted oaks also may arrive: and planted this tree must certainly have been, as will appear from what will be said farther concerning this area, when we enter on the antiquities of Selborne.

On the Blackmoor estate there is a small wood called Losel's, of a few acres, that was lately furnished with a set of oaks of a peculiar growth and great value; they were tall and taper like firs, but standing near together had very small heads, only a little brush without any large limbs. About twenty years ago the bridge at the Toy, near Hampton-court, being much decayed, some trees were wanted for the repairs that were fifty feet long without bough, and would measure twelve inches diameter at the little end. Twenty such trees did a purveyor find in this little wood, with this advantage, that many of them answered the description at sixty feet. These trees were sold for twenty pounds apiece.

In the centre of this grove there stood an oak, which, though shapely and tall on the whole, bulged out into a large excrescence about the middle of the stem. On this a pair of ravens had fixed their residence for such a series of years, that the oak was distinguished by the title of the Raven-tree. Many were the attempts of the neighbouring youths to get at this eyry: the difficulty whetted their inclinations, and each was ambitious of surmounting the arduous task. But, when they arrived at the swelling, it jutted out so in their way, and was so far beyond their grasp, that the most daring lads were awed, and acknowledged the undertaking to be too hazardous. So the ravens built on, nest upon nest, in perfect security, till the fatal day arrived in which the wood was to be levelled. It was in the month of February, when those birds usually sit. The saw was applied to the butt, the wedges were inserted into the opening, the woods echoed to the heavy blows of the beetle or mallet, the tree nodded to its fall; but still the dam sat on. At last, when it gave way, the bird was flung from her nest; and, though her parental affection deserved a better fate, was whipped down by the twigs, which brought her dead to the ground.

*   *   *

The fossil-shells of this district, and sorts of stone, such as have fallen within my observation, must not be passed over in silence. And first I must mention, as a great curiosity, a specimen that was ploughed up in the chalky fields, near the side of the down, and given to me for the singularity of its appearance, which, to an incurious eye, seems like a petrified fish of about four inches long, the *cardo* passing for an head and mouth. It is in reality a bivalve of the Linnæan genus of *Mytilus*, and the species of *Crista Galli*; called by Lister, *Rastellum*; by Rumphius, *Ostreum plicatum minus*; by D'Argenville, *Auris Porci*, s. *Crista Galli*, and by those who make collections *cock's comb*. Though I applied to several such in London, I could never meet with an entire specimen; nor could I ever find in books any engraving from a perfect one. In the superb museum at Leicester-house, permission was given me to examine for this article; and though I was disappointed as to the fossil, I was highly gratified with the sight of several of the shells themselves in high preservation. This bivalve is only known to inhabit the Indian Ocean, where it fixes itself to a zoophyte, known by the name *Gorgonia*. The curious foldings of the suture, the one into the other, the alternate flutings or grooves, and the curved form of my specimen being much easier expressed by the pencil than by words, I have caused it to be drawn and engraved.

Cornua Ammonis are very common about this village. As we were cutting an inclining path up the Hanger, the labourers found them frequently on that steep, just under the soil, in the chalk, and of a considerable size. In the lane above Well-head, in the way to Emshot, they abound in the bank, in a darkish sort of marl; and are usually very small and soft: but in Clay's Pond, a little farther on, at the end of the pit, where the soil is dug out for manure, I have occasionally observed them of large dimensions, perhaps fourteen or sixteen inches in diameter. But as these did not consist of firm stone, but were formed of a kind of *terra lapidosa*, or hardened clay, as soon as they were exposed to the rains and frost they mouldered away. These seemed as if they were a very recent production. In the chalk-pit, at the north-west end of the Hanger, large *nautili* are sometimes observed.

In the very thickest strata of our freestone, and at

considerable depths, well-diggers often find large scallops or *pectines*, having both shells deeply striated, and ridged and furrowed alternately. They are highly impregnated with, if not wholly composed of, the stone of the quarry.

*   *   *

As in a former letter the freestone of this place has been only mentioned incidentally, I shall here become more particular.

This stone is in great request for hearth-stones and the beds of ovens: and in lining of lime-kilns it turns to good account; for the workmen use sandy loam instead of mortar; the sand of which fluxes and runs by the intense heat, and so cases over the whole face of the kiln with a strong vitrified coat like glass, that it is well preserved from injuries of weather, and endures thirty or forty years. When chiseled smooth, it makes elegant fronts for houses, equal in colour and grain to the Bath stone; and superior in one respect, that, when seasoned, it does not scale. Decent chimney-pieces are worked from it of much closer and finer grain than Portland; and rooms are floored with it; but it proves rather too soft for this purpose. It is a freestone, cutting in all directions; yet has something of a grain parallel with the horizon, and therefore should not be surbedded, but laid in the same position as it grows in the quarry. On the ground abroad this firestone will not succeed for pavements, because, probably, some degree of saltness prevailing within it, the rain tears the slabs to pieces. Though this stone is too hard to be acted on by vinegar, yet both the white part, and even the blue rag, ferments strongly in mineral acids. Though the white stone will not bear wet, yet in every quarry at intervals there are thin strata of blue rag, which resist rain and frost; and are excellent for pitching of stables, paths, and courts, and for building of dry walls against banks, a valuable species of fencing, much in use in this village, and for mending of roads. This rag is rugged and stubborn, and will not hew to a smooth face; but is very durable: yet, as these strata are shallow and lie deep, large quantities cannot be procured but at considerable expense. Among the blue rags turn up some blocks tinged with a stain of yellow or rust colour, which seem to be nearly as lasting as the blue; and every now and then balls of a friable substance, like rust of iron, called rust balls.

In Wolmer-forest I see but one sort of stone, called by the workmen sand, or forest-stone. This is generally of the colour of rusty iron, and might probably be worked as iron ore; is very hard and heavy, and of a firm, compact texture, and composed of a small roundish crystalline grit, cemented together by a brown, terrene, ferruginous matter; will not cut without difficulty, nor easily strike fire with steel. Being often found in broad flat pieces, it makes good pavement for paths about houses, never becoming slippery in frost or rain; is excellent for dry walls, and is sometimes used in buildings. In many parts of that waste it lies scattered on the surface of the ground; but is dug on Weaver's-down, a vast hill on the eastern verge of that forest, where the pits are shallow, and the stratum thin. This stone is imperishable.

From a notion of rendering their work the more elegant, and giving it a finish, masons chip this stone into small fragments about the size of the head of a large nail; and then stick the pieces into the wet mortar along the joints of their freestone walls: this embellishment carries an odd appearance, and has occasioned strangers sometimes to ask us pleasantly, 'whether we fastened our walls together with tenpenny nails.'

*   *   *

Among the singularities of this place the two rocky hollow lanes, the one to Alton, and the other to the forest, deserve our attention. These roads, running through the malm lands, are, by the traffic of ages, and the fretting of water, worn down through the first stratum of our freestone, and partly through the second; so that they look more like water-courses than roads; and are bedded with naked rag for furlongs together. In many places they are reduced sixteen or eighteen feet beneath the level of the fields; and after floods, and in frosts, exhibit very grotesque and wild appearances, from the tangled roots that are twisted among the strata, and from the torrents rushing down their broken sides; and especially when those cascades are frozen into icicles, hanging in all the fanciful shapes of frost-work. These rugged gloomy scenes affright the ladies when they peep down into them from the paths above, and make timid horsemen shudder while they ride along them; but delight the naturalist with their various botany, and particularly with their curious *filices* with which they abound.

The manor of Selborne, was it strictly looked after, with its kindly aspects, and all its sloping coverts, would swarm with game; even now hares, partridges, and pheasants abound; and in old days woodcocks were as plentiful. There are few quails, because they more affect open fields than enclosures; after harvest some few landrails are seen.

The parish of Selborne, by taking in so much of the forest, is a vast district. Those who tread the bounds are employed part of three days in the business, and are of opinion that the outline, in all its curves and indentings, does not comprise less than thirty miles.

The village stands in a sheltered spot, secured by the Hanger from the strong westerly winds. The air is soft, but rather moist from the effluvia of so many trees; yet perfectly healthy and free from agues.

The quantity of rain that falls on it is very considerable, as may be supposed in so woody and mountainous a district. As my experience in measuring the water is but of short date, I am not qualified to give the mean quantity.*

I only know that:

	Inch.	Hund.
From May 1, 1779, the end of the year, there fell	28	37!
From Jan. 1, 1780, to Jan. 1, 1781, there fell. . .	27	32
From Jan. 1, 1781, to Jan. 1, 1782, there fell. . .	30	71

* A very intelligent gentleman assures me (and he speaks from upwards of forty years' experience) that the mean rain of any place cannot be ascertained till a person has measured it for a very long period. 'If I had only measured the rain,' says he, 'for the four first years, from 1740 to 1743, I should have said the mean rain at Lyndon was 16½ inches for the year; if from 1740 to 1750, 18½ inches. The mean rain before 1763 was 20¼; from 1763 and since, 25½; from 1770 to 1780, 26. If only 1773, 1774 and 1775 had been measured, Lyndon mean rain would have been called 32 inches.'

	Inch.	Hund.
From Jan. 1, 1782, to Jan. 1, 1783, there fell.	50	26!
From Jan. 1, 1783, to Jan. 1, 1784, there fell.	33	71
From Jan. 1, 1784, to Jan. 1, 1785, there fell.	33	80
From Jan. 1, 1785, to Jan. 1, 1786, there fell.	31	55
From Jan. 1, 1786, to Jan. 1, 1787, there fell.	39	57

The village of Selborne, and large hamlet of Oak-hanger, with the single farms, and many scattered houses along the verge of the forest, contain upwards of six hundred and seventy inhabitants.* We abound with poor; many of whom are sober and industrious, and live comfortably in good stone or brick cottages, which are glazed, and have chambers above stairs: mud buildings we have none. Besides the employment from husbandry the men work in hop gardens, of which we have many; and fell and bark timber. In the spring and summer the

---

* A STATE *of the* Parish *of* SELBORNE, *taken*
October 4, 1783.

The number of tenements or families, 136.

The number of inhabitants in the street is 313	Total, 676; near five inhabitants to each tenement.
In the rest of the parish. . . 363	

In the time of the Rev. Gilbert White, vicar, who died in 1727–8, the number of inhabitants was computed at about 500.

Average of baptisms for 60 years.

From 1720 to 1729, both years inclusive . . .	Males 6,9 / Females 6,0	12,9
From 1730 to 1739, both years inclusive	Males 8,2 / Females 7,1	15,3
From 1740 to 1749, inclusive	Males 9,2 / Females 6,6	15,8

From 1750 to 1759, inclusive	Males	7,6	15,7
	Females	8,1	
From 1760 to 1769, inclusive	Males	9,1	18,0
	Females	8,9	
From 1770 to 1779, inclusive	Males	10,5	20,3
	Females	9,8	

Total baptisms of Males   515 980
              Females   465

Total of baptisms from 1720 to 1779,
both inclusive, 60 years . . . 980.

Average of burials for 60 years.

From 1720 to 1729, both years inclusive . . .	Males	4,8	9,9
	Females	5,1	
From 1730 to 1739, both years inclusive. . . .	Males	4,8	10,6
	Females	5,8	
From 1740 to 1749, inclusive	Males	4,6	8,4
	Females	3,8	
From 1750 to 1759, inclusive	Males	4,9	10,0
	Females	5,1	
From 1760 to 1769, inclusive	Males	6,9	13,4
	Females	6,5	
From 1770 to 1779, inclusive	Males	5,5	11,7
	Females	6,2	

Total of burials of Males   315 640
              Females   325

Total of burials from 1720 to 1779
both inclusive, 60 years. 640.

Baptisms exceed burials by more than one-third.
Baptisms of Males exceed Females by one-tenth, or one in ten.
Burials of Females exceed Males by one in thirty.
It appears that a child, born and bred in this parish, has an equal
chance to live above forty years.
Twins thirteen times, many of whom dying young have lessened
the chance for life.
Chances for life in men and women appear to be equal.

women weed the corn; and enjoy a second harvest in September by hop-picking. Formerly, in the dead months they availed themselves greatly by spinning wool, for making of *barragons*, a genteel corded stuff, much in vogue at that time for summer wear; and chiefly manufactured at Alton, a neighbouring town, by some of the people called Quakers: but from circumstances this trade is at an end.* The inhabitants enjoy a good share of health and longevity: and the parish swarms with children.

*   *   *

Should I omit to describe with some exactness the forest of Wolmer, of which three-fifths perhaps lie in this parish, my account of Selborne would be very imperfect, as it is a district abounding with many curious productions, both animal and vegetable; and has often afforded me much entertainment both as a sportsman and as a naturalist.

The royal forest of Wolmer is a tract of land of about seven miles in length, by two and a half in breadth, running nearly from north to south, and is abutted on, to begin to the south, and so to proceed eastward, by the parishes of Greatham, Lysse, Rogate, and Trotton, in the county of Sussex; by Bramshot, Hedleigh, and Kingsley. This royalty consists entirely of sand covered with heath and fern; but is somewhat diversified with hills and dales, without having one standing tree in the whole extent. In the bottoms, where the waters stagnate, are many bogs, which formerly abounded with subterraneous trees; though Dr Plot says positively, that 'there never were any fallen trees hidden in the mosses of the southern counties.' But he was mistaken: for I myself

* Since the passage above was written, I am happy in being able to say that the spinning employment is a little revived, to the no small comfort of the industrious housewife.

A TABLE *of the* Baptisms, Burials, *and* Marriages, *from* January 2, 1761, *to* December 25, 1780, *in the* Parish *of* SELBORNE.

	BAPTISMS			BURIALS			MAR.
	Males.	Females.	Total.	Males.	Females.	Total.	
1761	8	10	18	2	4	6	3
1762	7	8	15	10	10	20	6
1763	8	10	18	3	4	7	5
1764	11	9	20	10	8	18	6
1765	12	6	18	9	7	16	6
1766	9	13	22	10	6	16	4
1767	14	5	19	6	5	11	2
1768	7	6	13	2	5	7	6
1769	9	14	23	6	5	11	2
1770	10	13	23	4	7	11	3
1771	10	6	16	3	4	7	4
1772	11	10	21	6	10	16	3
1773	8	5	13	7	5	12	3
1774	6	13	19	2	8	10	1
1775	20	7	27	13	8	21	6
1776	11	10	21	4	6	10	6
1777	8	13	21	7	2	9	4
1778	7	13	20	3	9	12	5
1779	14	8	22	5	6	11	5
1780	8	9	17	11	4	15	3
	198	188	386	123	123	246	83

During this period of twenty years the births of Males exceeded those of Females . . . 10.

The burials of each sex were equal.

And the births exceeded the deaths 140.

have seen cottages on the verge of this wild district, whose timbers consisted of a black hard wood, looking like oak, which the owners assured me they procured from the bogs by probing the soil with spits, or some such instruments: but the peat is so much cut out, and the moors have been so well examined, that none has been found of late. Besides the oak, I have also been shown pieces of fossil-wood of a paler colour, and softer nature, which the inhabitants called fir: but, upon a nice examination, and trial by fire, I could discover nothing resinous in them; and therefore rather suppose that they were parts of a willow or alder, or some such aquatic tree.

This lonely domain is a very agreeable haunt for many sorts of wild fowls, which not only frequent it in the winter, but breed there in the summer; such as lapwings, snipes, wild-ducks, and, as I have discovered within these few years, teals. Partridges in vast plenty are bred in good seasons on the verge of this forest, into which they love to make excursions: and in particular, in the dry summer of 1740 and 1741, and some years after, they swarmed to such a degree, that parties of unreasonable sportsmen killed twenty and sometimes thirty brace in a day.

But there was a nobler species of game in this forest, now extinct, which I have heard old people say abounded much before shooting flying became so common, and that was the heath-cock, black-game, or grouse. When I was a little boy I recollect one coming now and then to my father's table. The last pack remembered was killed about thirty-five years ago; and within these ten years one solitary greyhen was sprung by some beagles in beating for a hare. The sportsmen cried out, 'A hen pheasant'; but a gentleman present, who had often seen grouse in the north of England, assured me that it was a greyhen.

Nor does the loss of our black game prove the only gap in the *Fauna Selborniensis*; for another beautiful link in the chain of beings is wanting, I mean the red deer, which toward the beginning of this century amounted to about five hundred head, and made a stately appearance. There is an old keeper, now alive, named Adams, whose great-grandfather (mentioned in a perambulation taken in 1635), grandfather, father, and self, enjoyed the head keepership of Wolmer-forest in succession for more than an hundred years. This person assures me, that his father has often told him, that Queen Anne, as she was journeying on the Portsmouth road, did not think the forest of Wolmer beneath her royal regard. For she came out of the great road at Lippock, which is just by, and reposing herself on a bank smoothed for that purpose, lying about half a mile to the east of Wolmer-pond, and still called Queen's-bank, saw with great complacency and satisfaction the whole herd of red deer brought by the keepers along the vale before her, consisting then of about five hundred head. A sight this, worthy the attention of the greatest sovereign! But he further adds that, by means of the Waltham blacks, or, to use his own expression, as soon as they began *blacking*, they were reduced to about fifty head, and so continued decreasing till the time of the late Duke of Cumberland. It is now more than thirty years ago that his highness sent down an huntsman, and six yeoman-prickers, in scarlet jackets laced with gold, attended by the stag-hounds; ordering them to take every deer in this forest alive, and convey them in carts to Windsor. In the course of the summer they caught every stag, some of which showed extraordinary diversion; but, in the following winter, when the hinds were also carried off, such fine chases were exhibited as served the country people for matter of talk and wonder for years afterwards. I saw myself one of the yeoman-prickers single out a stag from the herd, and must confess that it was the most curious feat of activity I ever beheld, superior to anything in Mr Astley's riding-school. The exertions made by the horse and deer much exceeded all my expectations; though the former greatly excelled the latter in speed. When the devoted deer was separated from his companions, they gave him, by their watches, law, as they called it, for twenty minutes; when, sounding their horns, the stop-dogs were permitted to pursue, and a most gallant scene ensued.

*   *   *

On the verge of the forest, as it is now circumscribed, are three considerable lakes, two in Oakhanger, of which I have nothing particular to say; and one called Bin's or Bean's Pond, which is worthy the attention of a naturalist or a sportsman. For, being crowded at the upper end with willows, and with the *carex cespitosa*, it affords such a safe and pleasing shelter to wild-ducks, teals, snipes, etc., that they breed there. In the winter this covert is also frequented by foxes, and sometimes by pheasants; and the bogs produce many curious plants.

By a perambulation of Wolmer-forest and the Holt, made in 1635, and in the eleventh year of Charles the First (which now lies before me), it appears that the limits of the former are much circumscribed. For, to say nothing on the farther side, with which I am not so well acquainted, the bounds on this side, in old times, came into Binswood; and extended to the ditch of Ward le ham park, in which stands the curious mount called King John's Hill, and Lodge Hill; and to the verge of Hartley Mauduit, called Mauduit-hatch; comprehending also Short-heath, Oakhanger, and Oakwoods; a large district, now private property, though once belonging to the royal domain.

It is remarkable that the term *purlieu* is never once mentioned in this long roll of parchment. It contains, besides the perambulation, a rough estimate of the value of the timbers, which were considerable, growing at that time in the district of the Holt; and enumerates the officers, superior and inferior, of those joint forests, for the time being, and their ostensible fees and perquisites. In those days, as at present, there were hardly any trees in Wolmer-forest.

Within the present limits of the forest are three considerable lakes, Hogmer, Cranmer, and Wolmer; all of which are stocked with carp, tench, eels, and perch; but the fish do not thrive well, because the water is hungry, and the bottoms are a naked sand.

A circumstance respecting these ponds, though by no means peculiar to them, I cannot pass over in silence; and that is, that instinct by which in summer all the kine, whether oxen, cows, calves, or heifers, retire constantly to the water during the hotter hours; where, being more exempt from flies, and inhaling the coolness of that element, some belly deep, and some only to mid-leg, they ruminate and solace themselves from about ten in the morning till four in the afternoon, and then return to their feeding. During this great proportion of the day they drop much dung, in which insects nestle; and so supply food for the fish, which would be poorly subsisted but from this contingency. Thus nature, who is a great economist, converts the recreation of one animal to the support of another! Thomson, who is a nice observer of natural occurrences, did not let this pleasing circumstance escape him. He says, in his *Summer*:

> A various group the herds and flocks compose:
> . . . on the grassy bank
> Some ruminating lie; while others stand
> Half in the flood, and, often bending, sip
> The circling surface.

Wolmer-pond, so called, I suppose, for eminence sake, is a vast lake for this part of the world, containing, in its whole circumference, 2,646 yards, or very near a mile and a half. The length of the north-west and opposite side is about 704 yards, and the breadth of the south-west end about 456 yards. This measurement, which I caused to be made with good exactness, gives an area of about sixty-six acres, exclusive of a large irregular arm at the north-east corner, which we did not take into the reckoning.

On the face of this expanse of waters, and perfectly

secure from fowlers, lie all day long, in the winter season, vast flocks of ducks, teals, and widgeons, of various denominations; where they preen and solace, and rest themselves, till towards sunset, when they issue forth in little parties (for in their natural state they are all birds of the night) to feed in the brooks and meadows; returning again with the dawn of the morning. Had this lake an arm or two more, and were it planted round with thick covert (for now it is perfectly naked), it might make a valuable decoy.

Yet neither its extent, nor the clearness of its water, nor the resort of various and curious fowls, nor its picturesque groups of cattle, can render this *meer* so remarkable as the great quantity of coins that were found in its bed about forty years ago. But, as such discoveries more properly belong to the antiquities of this place, I shall suppress all particulars for the present, till I enter professedly on my series of letters respecting the more remote history of this village and district.

*   *   *

It has been my misfortune never to have had any neighbours whose studies have led them towards the pursuit of natural knowledge; so that, for want of a companion to quicken my industry and sharpen my attention, I have made but slender progress in a kind of information to which I have been attached from my childhood.

As to swallows (*hirundines rusticæ*) being found in a torpid state during the winter in the Isle of Wight, or any part of this country, I never heard any such account worth attending to. But a clergyman, of an inquisitive turn, assures me that, when he was a great boy, some workmen, in pulling down the battlements of a church tower early in the spring, found two or three swifts (*hirundines apodes*) among the rubbish, which were, at first appearance, dead, but, on being carried toward the fire, revived. He told me that, out of his great care to preserve them, he put them in a paper bag, and hung them by the kitchen fire, where they were suffocated.

Another intelligent person has informed me that, while he was a schoolboy at Brightelmstone, in Sussex, a great fragment of the chalk cliff fell down one stormy winter on the beach; and that many people found swallows among the rubbish; but, on my questioning him whether he saw any of those birds himself, to my no small disappointment, he answered me in the negative; but that others assured him they did.

Young broods of swallows began to appear this year on July the eleventh, and young martins (*hirundines urbicæ*) were then fledged in their nests. Both species will breed again once. For I see by my *Fauna* of last year, that young broods come forth so late as September the eighteenth. Are not these late hatchings more in favour of hiding than migration? Nay, some young martins remained in their nests last year so late as September the twenty-ninth; and yet they totally disappeared with us by the fifth of October.

How strange is it that the swift, which seems to live exactly the same life with the swallow and house-martin, should leave us before the middle of August invariably! while the latter stay often till the middle of October; and once I saw numbers of house-martins on the seventh of

November. The martins and red-wing fieldfares were flying in sight together; an uncommon assemblage of summer and winter birds.

A little yellow bird (it is either a species of the *alauda trivialis*, or rather perhaps of the *motacilla trochilus*) still continues to make a sibilous shivering noise in the tops of tall woods. The *stoparola* of Ray (for which we have as yet no name in these parts) is called, in your *Zoology*, the fly-catcher. There is one circumstance characteristic of this bird, which seems to have escaped observation, and that is, that it takes its stand on the top of some stake or post, from whence it springs forth on its prey, catching a fly in the air, and hardly ever touching the ground, but returning still to the same stand for many times together.

I perceive there are more than one species of the *motacilla trochilus*: Mr Derham supposes, in Ray's *Philos. Letters*, that he has discovered three. In these there is again an instance of some very common birds that have as yet no English name.

Mr Stillingfleet makes a question whether the black-cap (*motacilla atricapilla*) be a bird of passage or not: I think there is no doubt of it: for, in April, in the very first fine weather, they come trooping, all at once, into these parts, but are never seen in the winter. They are delicate songsters.

Numbers of snipes breed every summer in some moory ground on the verge of this parish. It is very amusing to see the cock bird on wing at that time, and to hear his piping and humming notes.

I have had no opportunity yet of procuring any of

those mice which I mentioned to you in town. The person that brought me the last says they are plenty in harvest, at which time I will take care to get more; and will endeavour to put the matter out of doubt, whether it be a nondescript species or not.

I suspect much there may be two species of water-rats. Ray says, and Linnæus after him, that the water-rat is web-footed behind. Now I have discovered a rat on the banks of our little stream that is not web-footed, and yet is an excellent swimmer and diver: it answers exactly to the *mus amphibius* of Linnæus (see *Syst. Nat.*), which he says '*natat in fossis et urinatur.*' I should be glad to procure one '*plantis palmatis.*' Linnæus seems to be in a puzzle about his *mus amphibius*, and to doubt whether it differs from his *mus terrestris*; which if it be, as he allows, the '*mus agrestis capite grandi brachyuros*' of Ray, is widely different from the water-rat, both in size, make, and manner of life.

As to the *falco*, which I mentioned in town, I shall take the liberty to send it down to you into Wales; presuming on your candour, that you will excuse me if it should appear as familiar to you as it is strange to me. Though mutilated '*qualem dices . . . antehac fuisse, tales cum sint reliquiæ!*'

It haunted a marshy piece of ground in quest of wild-ducks and snipes: but, when it was shot, had just knocked down a rook, which it was tearing in pieces. I cannot make it answer to any of our English hawks; neither could I find any like it at the curious exhibition of stuffed birds in Spring-gardens. I found it nailed up at the end of a barn, which is the countryman's museum.

The parish I live in is a very abrupt, uneven country, full of hills and woods, and therefore full of birds.

*   *   *

It will not be without impatience, that I shall wait for your thoughts with regard to the *falco*; as to its weight, breadth, etc., I wish I had set them down at the time; but, to the best of my remembrance, it weighed two pounds and eight ounces, and measured, from wing to wing, thirty-eight inches. Its cere and feet were yellow, and the circle of its eyelids bright yellow. As it had been killed some days, and the eyes were sunk, I could make no good observation on the colour of the pupils and the irides.

The most unusual birds I ever observed in these parts were a pair of hoopoes (*upupa*) which came several years ago in the summer, and frequented an ornamented piece of ground, which joins to my garden, for some weeks. They used to march about in a stately manner, feeding in the walks, many times in the day; and seemed disposed to breed in my outlet; but were frightened and persecuted by idle boys, who would never let them be at rest.

Three gross-beaks (*loxia coccothraustes*) appeared some years ago in my fields, in the winter; one of which I shot: since that, now and then one is occasionally seen in the same dead season.

A cross-bill (*loxia curvirostra*) was killed last year in this neighbourhood.

Our streams, which are small, and rise only at the end of the village, yield nothing but the bull's head or miller's thumb (*gobius fluviatilis capitatus*), the trout (*trutta fluviatilis*), the eel (*anguilla*), the lampern (*lampætra parva et fluviatilis*), and the stickle-back (*pisciculus aculeatus*).

We are twenty miles from the sea, and almost as many from a great river, and therefore see but little of sea-birds. As to wild fowls, we have a few teams of ducks bred in the moors where the snipes breed; and multitudes of widgeons and teals in hard weather frequent our lakes in the forest.

Having some acquaintance with a tame brown owl, I find that it casts up the fur of mice, and the feathers of birds in pellets, after the manner of hawks: when full, like a dog, it hides what it cannot eat.

The young of the barn-owl are not easily raised, as they want a constant supply of fresh mice: whereas the young of the brown owl will eat indiscriminately all that is brought; snails, rats, kittens, puppies, magpies, and any kind of carrion or offal.

The house-martins have eggs still, and squab-young. The last swift I observed was about the twenty-first of August; it was a straggler.

Red-starts, fly-catchers, white-throats, and *reguli non cristati*, still appear; but I have seen no black-caps lately.

I forgot to mention that I once saw, in Christ Church College quadrangle in Oxford, on a very sunny warm morning, a house-martin flying about, and settling on the parapet, so late as the twentieth of November.

At present I know only two species of bats, the common *vespertilio murinus* and the *vespertilio auritus*.

I was much entertained last summer with a tame bat, which would take flies out of a person's hand. If you gave it anything to eat, it brought its wings round before the mouth, hovering and hiding its head in the manner of birds of prey when they feed. The adroitness it showed in shearing off the wings of the flies, which were always rejected, was worthy of observation, and pleased me much. Insects seem to be most acceptable, though it did not refuse raw flesh when offered: so that the notion that bats go down chimneys and gnaw men's bacon, seems no improbable story. While I amused myself with this wonderful quadruped, I saw it several times confute the vulgar opinion, that bats when down on a flat surface cannot get on the wing again, by rising with great ease from the floor. It ran, I observed, with more dispatch than I was aware of; but in a most ridiculous and grotesque manner.

Bats drink on the wing, like swallows, by sipping the surface, as they play over pools and streams. They love to frequent waters, not only for the sake of drinking, but on account of insects, which are found over them in the greatest plenty. As I was going, some years ago, pretty late, in a boat from Richmond to Sunbury, on a warm summer's evening, I think I saw myriads of bats between the two places: the air swarmed with them all along the Thames, so that hundreds were in sight at a time.

*　　*　　*

It gave me no small satisfaction to hear that the *falco* turned out an uncommon one. I must confess I should have been better pleased to have heard that I had sent you a bird that you had never seen before; but that, I find, would be a difficult task.

I have procured some of the mice mentioned in my

former letters, a young one and a female with young, both of which I have preserved in brandy. From the colour, shape, size, and manner of nesting, I make no doubt but that the species is nondescript. They are much smaller and more slender than the *mus domesticus medius* of Ray; and have more of the squirrel or dormouse colour: their belly is white, a straight line along their sides divides the shades of their back and belly. They never enter into houses; are carried into ricks and barns with the sheaves; abound in harvest, and build their nests amidst the straws of the corn above the ground, and sometimes in thistles. They breed as many as eight at a litter, in a little round nest composed of the blades of grass or wheat.

One of these nests I procured this autumn, most artificially platted, and composed of the blades of wheat; perfectly round, and about the size of a cricket-ball; with the aperture so ingeniously closed, that there was no discovering to what part it belonged. It was so compact and well filled, that it would roll across the table without being discomposed, though it contained eight little mice that were naked and blind. As this nest was perfectly full, how could the dam come at her litter respectively so as to administer a teat to each? perhaps she opens different places for that purpose, adjusting them again when the business is over: but she could not possibly be contained herself in the ball with her young, which moreover would be daily increasing in bulk. This wonderful pro-creant cradle, an elegant instance of the efforts of instinct, was found in a wheat-field, suspended in the head of a thistle.

A gentleman, curious in birds, wrote me word that his servant had shot one last January, in that severe weather, which he believed would puzzle me. I called to see it this summer, not knowing what to expect: but, the moment I took it in hand, I pronounced it the male *garrulus bohemicus* or German silk-tail, from the five peculiar crimson tags or points which it carries at the end of five of the short remiges. It cannot, I suppose, with any propriety, be called an English bird: and yet I see, by Ray's *Philosoph. Letters*, that great flocks of them, feeding upon haws, appeared in this kingdom in the winter of 1685.

The mention of haws put me in mind that there is a total failure of that wild fruit, so conducive to the support of many of the winged nation. For the same severe weather, late in the spring, which cut off all the produce of the more tender and curious trees, destroyed also that of the more hardy and common.

Some birds, haunting with the missel-thrushes, and feeding on the berries of the yew-tree, which answered to the description of the *merula torquata*, or ring-ousel, were lately seen in this neighbourhood. I employed some people to procure me a specimen, but without success.

Query. – Might not canary birds be naturalized to this climate, provided their eggs were put in the spring, into the nests of some of their congeners, as goldfinches, greenfinches, etc.? Before winter perhaps they might be hardened, and able to shift for themselves.

About ten years ago I used to spend some weeks yearly at Sunbury, which is one of those pleasant villages lying on the Thames, near Hampton-court. In the autumn, I could not help being much amused with those myriads of the swallow kind which assemble in those parts. But what struck me most was, that, from the time they began to congregate, forsaking the chimneys and houses, they roosted every night in the osier-beds of the aits of that river. Now this resorting towards that element, at that season of the year, seems to give some countenance to the northern opinion (strange as it is) of their retiring under water. A Swedish naturalist is so much persuaded of that fact, that he talks, in his calendar of *Flora*, as familiarly of the swallows going under water in the beginning of September, as he would of his poultry going to roost a little before sunset.

An observing gentleman in London writes me word that he saw a house-martin, on the twenty-third of last October, flying in and out of its nest in the Borough. And I myself, on the twenty-ninth of last October (as I was travelling through Oxford), saw four or five swallows hovering round and settling on the roof of the county-hospital.

Now is it likely that these poor little birds (which perhaps had not been hatched but a few weeks) should, at that late season of the year, and from so midland a county, attempt a voyage to Goree or Senegal, almost as far as the equator.

I acquiesce entirely in your opinion – that, though most of the swallow kind may migrate, yet that some do stay behind and hide with us during the winter.

As to the short-winged soft-billed birds, which come trooping in such numbers in the spring, I am at a loss even what to suspect about them. I watched them narrowly this year, and saw them abound till about Michaelmas, when they appeared no longer. Subsist they cannot openly among us, and yet elude the eyes of the inquisitive: and, as to their hiding, no man pretends to have found any of them in a torpid state in the winter. But with regard to their migration, what difficulties attend that supposition! that such feeble bad fliers (who the summer long never flit but from hedge to hedge) should be able to traverse vast seas and continents in order to enjoy milder seasons amidst the regions of Africa!

*   *   *

As in one of your former letters you expressed the more satisfaction from my correspondence on account of my living in the most southerly county; so now I may return the compliment, and expect to have my curiosity gratified by your living much more to the north.

For many years past I have observed that towards Christmas vast flocks of chaffinches have appeared in the fields; many more, I used to think, than could be hatched in any one neighbourhood. But, when I came to observe them more narrowly, I was amazed to find that they seemed to be almost all hens. I communicated my suspicions to some intelligent neighbours, who, after taking pains about the matter, declared that they also thought them all mostly females; at least fifty to one. This extraordinary occurrence brought to my mind the remark of Linnæus; that 'before winter, all their hen chaffinches migrate through Holland into Italy.' Now I want to know, from some curious person in the north, whether there are any large flocks of these finches with them in the winter, and of which sex they mostly consist? For, from such intelligence, one might be able to judge whether our female flocks migrate from the other end of the island, or whether they come over to us from the continent.

We have, in the winter, vast flocks of the common linnets; more, I think, than can be bred in any one district. These, I observe, when the spring advances, assemble on some tree in the sunshine, and join all in a gentle sort of chirping, as if they were about to-break up their winter quarters and betake themselves to their proper summer homes. It is well known, at least, that the swallows and the fieldfares do congregate with a gentle twittering before they make their respective departure.

You may depend on it that the bunting, *emberiza miliaria*, does not leave this country in the winter. In January 1767 I saw several dozen of them, in the midst of a severe frost, among the bushes on the downs near Andover: in our woodland enclosed district it is a rare bird.

Wagtails, both white and yellow, are with us all the winter. Quails crowd to our southern coast, and are often killed in numbers by people that go on purpose.

Mr Stillingfleet, in his Tracts, says that 'if the wheatear (*œanthe*) does not quit England, it certainly shifts places; for about harvest they are not to be found, where there was before great plenty of them.' This well accounts for the vast quantities that are caught about that time on the south downs near Lewes, where they are esteemed a delicacy. There have been shepherds, I have been credibly informed, that have made many pounds in a season by catching them in traps. And though such multitudes are taken, I never saw (and I am well acquainted with those parts) above two or three at a time: for they are never gregarious. They may, perhaps, migrate in general; and, for that purpose, draw towards the coast of Sussex in autumn; but that they do not all withdraw I am sure; because I see a few stragglers in many counties, at all times of the year, especially about warrens and stone quarries.

I have no acquaintance, at present, among the gentlemen of the navy: but have written to a friend, who was a sea-chaplain in the late war, desiring him to look into his minutes, with respect to birds that settled on their rigging during their voyage up or down the channel. What Hasselquist says on that subject is remarkable: there were little short-winged birds frequently coming on board his ship all the way from our channel quite up to the Levant, especially before squally weather.

What you suggest, with regard to Spain, is highly probable. The winters of Andalusia are so mild, that, in all likelihood, the soft-billed birds that leave us at that season may find insects sufficient to support them there.

Some young man, possessed of fortune, health, and leisure, should make an autumnal voyage into that kingdom; and should spend a year there, investigating the natural history of that vast country. Mr Willughby passed through that kingdom on such an errand; but he seems to have skirted along in a superficial manner and an ill humour, being much disgusted at the rude, dissolute manners of the people.

I have no friend left now at Sunbury to apply to about the swallows roosting on the aits of the Thames: nor can I hear any more about those birds which I suspected were *merulæ torquatæ*.

As to the small mice, I have farther to remark, that though they hang their nests for breeding up amidst the straws of the standing corn, above the ground; yet I find that, in the winter, they burrow deep in the earth, and make warm beds of grass: but their grand rendezvous seems to be in corn-ricks, into which they are carried at harvest. A neighbour housed an oat-rick lately, under the thatch of which were assembled near an hundred, most of which were taken; and some I saw. I measured them; and found that, from nose to tail, they were just two inches and a quarter, and their tails just two inches long. Two of them, in a scale, weighed down just one copper half-penny, which is about a third of an ounce avoirdupois: so that I suppose they are the smallest quadrupeds in this island. A full-grown *mus medius domesticus* weighs, I find, one ounce, lumping weight, which is more than six times as much as the mouse above; and measures from nose to rump four inches and a quarter, and the same in its tail.

We have had a very severe frost and deep snow this month. My thermometer was one day fourteen degrees and a half below the freezing point, within doors. The tender evergreens were injured pretty much. It was very providential that the air was still, and the ground well covered with snow, else vegetation in general must have suffered prodigiously. There is reason to believe that some days were more severe than any since the year 1739–40.

*   *   *

The history of the stone curlew, *charadrius œdicnemus* is as follows. It lays its eggs, usually two, never more than three, on the bare ground, without any nest, in the field; so that the countryman, in stirring his fallows, often destroys them. The young run immediately from the egg like partridges, etc., and are withdrawn to some flinty field by their dam, where they skulk among the stones, which are their best security; for their feathers are so exactly of the colour of our grey spotted flints, that the most exact observer, unless he catches the eye of the young bird, may be eluded. The eggs are short and round; of a dirty white, spotted with dark bloody blotches. Though I might not be able, just when I pleased, to procure you a bird, yet I could show you them almost any day; and any evening you may hear them round the village, for they make a clamour which may be heard a mile. *Œdicnemus* is a most apt and expressive name for them, since their legs seem swoln like those of a gouty man. After harvest I have shot them before the pointers in turnip-fields.

I make no doubt but there are three species of the willow-wrens: two I know perfectly; but have not been able yet to procure the third. No two birds can differ more in their notes, and that constantly, than those two that I am acquainted with; for the one has a joyous, easy, laughing note; the other a harsh loud chirp.

The former is every way larger, and three-quarters of an inch longer, and weighs two drams and a half; while the latter weighs but two: so the songster is one-fifth heavier than the chirper. The chirper (being the first summer-bird of passage that is heard, the wryneck sometimes excepted) begins his two notes in the middle of March, and continues them through the spring and summer till the end of August, as appears by my journals. The legs of the larger of these two are flesh-coloured; of the less, black.

The grasshopper-lark began his sibilous note in my fields last Saturday. Nothing can be more amusing than the whisper of this little bird, which seems to be close by though at an hundred yards distance; and, when close at your ear, is scarce any louder than when a great way off. Had I not been a little acquainted with insects, and known that the grasshopper kind is not yet hatched, I should have hardly believed but that it had been a *locusta* whispering in the bushes. The country people laugh when you tell them that it is the note of a bird. It is a most artful creature, skulking in the thickest part of a bush; and will sing at a yard distance, provided it be concealed. I was obliged to get a person to go on the other side of the hedge where it haunted; and then it would run, creeping like a mouse, before us for a hundred yards together, through the bottom of the thorns; yet it would not come into fair sight: but in a morning early, and when undisturbed, it sings on the top of a twig, gaping and shivering with its wings. Mr Ray himself had no knowledge of this bird, but received his account from Mr Johnson, who apparently confounds it with the *reguli non cristati*, from which it is very distinct. See Ray's *Philosophical Letters*, p. 108.

A LIST *of the* SUMMER BIRDS *of* PASSAGE *discovered in this neighbourhood, ranged somewhat in the Order in which they appear:*

	Linnæi Nomina.
Smallest willow-wren,	*Motacilla trochilus.*
Wryneck,	*Jynx torquilla.*
House-swallow,	*Hirundo rustica.*
Martin,	*Hirundo urbica.*
Sand-martin,	*Hirundo riparia.*
Cuckoo,	*Cuculus canorus.*
Nightingale,	*Motacilla luscinia.*
Black-cap,	*Motacilla atricapilla.*
White-throat,	*Motacilla sylvia.*
Middle willow-wren,	*Motacilla trochilus.*
Swift,	*Hirundo apus.*
Stone curlew?	*Charadrius œdicnemus?*
Turtle-dove?	*Turtur aldrovandi?*
Grasshopper-lark,	*Alauda trivialis.*
Landrail,	*Rallus crex.*
Largest willow-wren,	*Motacilla trochilus.*
Redstart,	*Motacilla phænicurus.*
Goat-sucker, or fern-owl,	*Caprimulgus europæus.*
Fly-catcher,	*Muscicapa grisola.*

The fly-catcher (*stoparola*) has not yet appeared: it usually breeds in my vine. The redstart begins to sing: its note is short and imperfect, but is continued till about the middle of June. The willow-wrens (the smaller sort) are horrid pests in a garden, destroying the pease, cherries, currants, etc., and are so tame that a gun will not scare them.

My countrymen talk much of a bird that makes a clatter with its bill against a dead bough, or some old pales, calling it a jar-bird. I procured one to be shot in the very fact; it proved to be the *sitta europæa* (the nut-hatch). Mr Ray says that the less spotted woodpecker does the same. This noise may be heard a furlong or more.

Now is the only time to ascertain the short-winged summer birds; for, when the leaf is out, there is no making any remarks on such a restless tribe; and, when once the young begin to appear, it is all confusion: there is no distinction of genus, species, or sex.

In breeding-time snipes play over the moors, piping and humming: they always hum as they are descending. Is not their hum ventriloquous like that of a turkey? Some suspect it is made by their wings.

This morning I saw the golden-crowned wren, whose crown glitters like burnished gold. It often hangs like a tit-mouse, with its back downwards.

*   *   *

It is, I find, in zoology as it is in botany: all nature is so full, that that district produces the greatest variety which is the most examined. Several birds, which are said to belong to the north only, are, it seems, often in the south. I have discovered this summer three species of birds with us, which writers mention as only to be seen in the northern counties. The first that was brought me (on the 14th of May) was the sandpiper, *tringa hypoleucus*:

it was a cock bird, and haunted the banks of some ponds near the village; and, as it had a companion, doubtless intended to have bred near that water. Besides, the owner has told me since, that, on recollection, he has seen some of the same birds round his ponds in former summers.

The next bird that I procured (on the 21st of May) was a male red-backed butcher bird, *lanius collurio*. My neighbour, who shot it, says that it might easily have escaped his notice, had not the outcries and chattering of the white-throats and other small birds drawn his attention to the bush where it was: its craw was filled with the legs and wings of beetles.

The next rare birds (which were procured for me last week) were some ring-ousels, *turdi jorquati*.

This week twelve months a gentleman from London, being with us, was amusing himself with a gun, and found, he told us, on an old yew hedge where there were berries, some birds like blackbirds, with rings of white round their necks: a neighbouring farmer also at the same time observed the same; but, as no specimens were procured little notice was taken. I mentioned this circumstance to you in my letter of November the 4th, 1767 (you, however, paid but small regard to what I said, as I had not seen these birds myself); but last week, the aforesaid farmer, seeing a large flock, twenty or thirty of these birds, shot two cocks and two hens: and says, on recollection, that he remembers to have observed these birds again last spring, about Lady-day, as it were, on their return to the north. Now perhaps these ousels are not the ousels of the north of England, but belong to the more northern parts of Europe; and may retire before the excessive rigour of the frosts in those parts; and return to breed in the spring, when the cold abates. If this be the case, here is discovered a new bird of winter passage, concerning whose migrations the writers are silent: but if these birds should prove the ousels of the north of England, then here is a migration disclosed within our own kingdom never before remarked. It does not yet appear whether they retire beyond the bounds of our island to the south; but it is most probable that they usually do, or else one cannot suppose that they would have continued so long unnoticed in the southern counties. The ousel is larger than a blackbird, and feeds on haws; but last autumn (when there were no haws) it fed on yew-berries: in the spring it feeds on ivy-berries, which ripen only at that season, in March and April.

I must not omit to tell you (as you have been so lately on the study of reptiles) that my people, every now and then of late, draw up with a bucket of water from my well, which is 63 feet deep, a large black warty lizard with a fin-tail and yellow belly. How they first came down at that depth, and how they were ever to have got out thence without help, is more than I am able to say.

My thanks are due to you for your trouble and care in the examination of a buck's head. As far as your discoveries reach at present, they seem much to corroborate my suspicions; and I hope Mr — may find reason to give his decision in my favour; and then, I think, we may advance this extraordinary provision of nature as a new instance of the wisdom of God in the creation.

As yet I have not quite done with my history of the

œdicnemus, or stone curlew; for I shall desire a gentleman in Sussex (near whose house these birds congregate in vast flocks in the autumn) to observe nicely when they leave him (if they do leave him), and when they return again in the spring; I was with this gentleman lately, and saw several single birds.

*   *   *

As to the peculiarity of jackdaws building with us under the ground in rabbit-burrows, you have, in part, hit upon the reason; for, in reality, there are hardly any towers or steeples in all this country. And perhaps, Norfolk excepted, Hampshire and Sussex are as meanly furnished with churches as almost any counties in the kingdom. We have many livings of two or three hundred pounds a year, whose houses of worship make little better appearance than dovecots. When I first saw Northamptonshire, Cambridgeshire and Huntingdonshire, and the fens of Lincolnshire, I was amazed at the number of spires which presented themselves in every point of view. As an admirer of prospects, I have reason to lament this want in my own country; for such objects are very necessary ingredients in an elegant landscape.

What you mention with respect to reclaimed toads raises my curiosity. An ancient author, though no naturalist, has well remarked that 'Every kind of beasts, and of birds, and of serpents, and of things in the sea, is tamed, and hath been tamed, of mankind.'

It is a satisfaction to me to find that a green lizard has actually been procured for you in Devonshire; because it corroborates my discovery, which I made many years ago, of the same sort, on a sunny sandbank near Farnham in Surrey. I am well acquainted with the south hams of Devonshire; and can suppose that district, from its southerly situation, to be a proper habitation for such animals in their best colours.

Since the ring-ousels of your vast mountains do certainly not forsake them against winter, our suspicions that those which visit this neighbourhood about Michaelmas are not English birds, but driven from the more northern parts of Europe by the frosts, are still more reasonable: and it will be worth your pains to endeavour to trace from whence they come, and to inquire why they make so very short a stay.

In your account of your error with regard to the two species of herons, you incidentally gave me great entertainment in your description of the heronry at Cressi-hall; which is a curiosity I could never manage to see. Four-score nests of such a bird on one tree is a rarity which I would ride half as many miles to have a sight of. Pray be sure to tell me in your next whose seat Cressi-hall is, and near what town it lies. I have often thought that those vast extents of fens have never been sufficiently explored. If half a dozen gentlemen, furnished with a good strength of water-spaniels, were to beat them over for a week, they would certainly find more species.

There is no bird, I believe, whose manners I have studied more than that of the *caprimulgus* (the goat-sucker), as it is a wonderful and curious creature: but I have always found that though sometimes it may chatter as it flies, as I know it does, yet in general it utters its jarring note sitting on a bough; and I have for many an half hour watched it as it sat with its under mandible quivering, and particularly this summer. It perches usually on a bare twig, with its head lower than its tail, in an attitude well expressed by your draughtsman in the folio *British Zoology*. This bird is most punctual in beginning its song exactly at the close of day; so exactly that I have known it strike up more than once or twice just at the report of the Portsmouth evening gun, which we can hear when the weather is still. It appears to me past all doubt that its notes are formed by organic impulse, by the powers of the parts of its windpipe, formed for sound, just as cats pur. You will credit me, I hope, when I tell you that, as my neighbours were assembled in an hermitage on the side of a steep hill where we drink tea, one of these churn-owls came and settled on the cross of that little straw edifice and began to chatter, and continued his note for many minutes: and we were all struck with wonder to find that the organs of that little animal, when put in motion, gave a sensible vibration to the whole building! This bird also sometimes makes a small squeak, repeated four or five times; and I have observed that to happen when the cock has been pursuing the hen in a toying way through the boughs of a tree.

It would not be at all strange if your bat, which you have procured, should prove a new one, since five species have been found in a neighbouring kingdom. The great sort that I mentioned is certainly a nondescript: I saw but one this summer, and that I had no opportunity of taking.

Your account of the Indian-grass was entertaining. I am no angler myself; but inquiring of those that are, what they supposed that part of their tackle to be made of? they replied 'of the intestines of a silkworm.'

Though I must not pretend to great skill in entomology, yet I cannot say that I am ignorant of that kind of knowledge: I may now and then, perhaps, be able to furnish you with a little information.

The vast rains ceased with us much about the same time as with you, and since we have had delicate weather. Mr Barker, who has measured the rain for more than thirty years, says, in a late letter, that more has fallen this year than in any he ever attended to; though, from July 1763 to January 1764, more fell than in any seven months of this year.

★   ★   ★

It gives me satisfaction to find that my account of the ousel migration pleases you. You put a very shrewd question when you ask me how I know that their autumnal migration is southward? Was not candour and openness the very life of natural history, I should pass over this query just as the sly commentator does over a crabbed passage in a classic; but common ingenuousness obliges me to confess, not without some degree of shame, that I only reasoned in that case from analogy. For as all other autumnal birds migrate from the northward to us, to partake of our milder winters, and return to the northward again when the rigorous cold abates, so I concluded that the ring-ousels did the same, as well as their congeners the fieldfares; and especially

44

as ring-ousels are known to haunt cold mountainous countries: but I have good reason to suspect since that they may come to us from westward; because I hear, from very good authority, that they breed on Dartmoor; and that they forsake that wild district about the time that our visitors appear, and do not return till late in the spring.

I have taken a great deal of pains about your *salicaria* and mine, with a white stroke over its eye, and a tawny rump. I have surveyed it alive and dead, and have procured several specimens; and am perfectly persuaded myself (and trust you will soon be convinced of the same) that it is no more nor less than the *passer arundinaceus minor* of Ray. This bird, by some means or other, seems to be entirely omitted in the *British Zoology*; and one reason probably was because it is so strangely classed in Ray, who ranges it among his *picis affines*. It ought no doubt to have gone among his *aviculæ caudâ unicolore*, and among your slender-billed small birds of the same division. Linnæus might with great propriety have put it into his genus of *motacilla*; and the *motacilla salicaria* of his *Fauna Suecica* seems to come the nearest to it. It is no uncommon bird, haunting the sides of ponds and rivers where there is covert, and the reeds and sedges of moors. The country people in some places call it the sedge-bird. It sings incessantly night and day during the breeding-time, imitating the note of a sparrow, a swallow, a sky-lark; and has a strange hurrying manner in its song. My specimens correspond most minutely to the description of your fen *salicaria*, shot near Revesby. Mr Ray has given an excellent characteristic of it when he says, '*Rostrum & pedes in hâc aviculâ multò majores sunt quàm pro corporis ratione.*' See letter May 29, 1769.

I have got you the egg of an *œdicnemus*, or stone curlew, which was picked up in a fallow on the naked ground: there were two; but the finder inadvertently crushed one with his foot before he saw them.

When I wrote to you last year on reptiles, I wish I had not forgot to mention the faculty that snakes have of stinking *se defendendo*. I knew a gentleman who kept a tame snake, which was in its person as sweet as any animal while in a good humour and unalarmed; but as soon as a stranger or a dog or cat, came in, it fell to hissing, and filled the room with such nauseous effluvia as rendered it hardly supportable. Thus the squnck, or stonck, of Ray's *Synop. Quadr.* is an innocuous and sweet animal; but, when pressed hard by dogs and men, it can eject such a pestilent and fetid smell and excrement, that nothing can be more horrible.

A gentleman sent me lately a fine specimen of the *lanius minor cinerascens cum maculâ in scapulis albâ Raii*; which is a bird that, at the time of your publishing your two first volumes of *British Zoology*, I find you had not seen. You have described it well from Edwards's drawing.

*   *   *

Last month we had such a series of cold turbulent weather, such a constant succession of frost, and snow, and hail, and tempest, that the regular migration or appearance of the summer birds was much interrupted. Some did not show themselves (at least were not heard) till weeks after their usual time; as the black-cap and white-throat; and some have not been heard yet, as the grasshopper-lark and largest willow-wren. As to the fly-catcher, I have not seen it; it is indeed one of the latest, but should appear about this time: and yet, amidst all this meteorous strife and war of the elements, two swallows discovered themselves as long ago as the eleventh of April, in frost and snow; but they withdrew quickly, and were not visible again for many days. House-martins, which are always more backward than swallows, were not observed till May came in.

Among the monogamous birds several are to be found, after pairing-time, single, and of each sex: but whether this state of celibacy is matter of choice or necessity, is not so easily discoverable. When the house-sparrows deprive my martins of their nests, as soon as I cause one to be shot, the other, be it cock or hen, presently procures a mate, and so for several times following.

I have known a dove-house infested by a pair of white owls, which made great havoc among the young pigeons: one of the owls was shot as soon as possible; but the survivor readily found a mate, and the mischief went on. After some time the new pair were both destroyed, and the annoyance ceased.

Another instance I remember of a sportsman, whose zeal for the increase of his game being greater than his humanity, after pairing-time he always shot the cock-bird of every couple of partridges upon his grounds; supposing that the rivalry of many males interrupted the breed: he used to say, that, though he had widowed the same hen several times, yet he found she was still provided with a fresh paramour, that did not take her away from her usual haunt.

Again; I knew a lover of setting, an old sportsman, who has often told me that soon after harvest he has frequently taken small coveys of partridges, consisting of cock-birds alone; these he pleasantly used to call old bachelors.

There is a propensity belonging to common house-cats that is very remarkable; I mean their violent fondness for fish, which appears to be their most favourite food: and yet nature in this instance seems to have planted in them an appetite that, unassisted, they know not how to gratify: for of all quadrupeds cats are the least disposed towards water; and will not, when they can avoid it, deign to wet a foot, much less to plunge into that element.

Quadrupeds that prey on fish are amphibious: such is the otter, which by nature is so well formed for diving, that it makes great havoc among the inhabitants of the waters. Not supposing that we had any of those beasts in our shallow brooks, I was much pleased to see a male otter brought to me, weighing twenty-one pounds, that had been shot on the bank of our stream below the Priory, where the rivulet divides the parish of Selborne from Harteley-wood.

*　　*　　*

The French, I think, in general, are strangely prolix in their natural history. What Linnæus says with respect to insects holds good in every other branch: '*Verbositas præsentis sæculi, calamitas artis.*'

Pray how do you approve of Scopoli's new work? As I admire his *Entomologia*, I long to see it.

I forgot to mention in my last letter (and had not room to insert in the former) that the male moose, in rutting time, swims from island to island, in the lakes and rivers of North America, in pursuit of the females. My friend, the chaplain, saw one killed in the water as it was on that errand in the river St Lawrence: it was a monstrous beast, he told me; but he did not take the dimensions.

When I was last in town our friend Mr Barrington most obligingly carried me to see many curious sights. As you were then writing to him about horns, he carried me to see many strange and wonderful specimens. There is, I remember, at Lord Pembroke's, at Wilton, an horn room furnished with more than thirty different pairs; but I have not seen that house lately.

Mr Barrington showed me many astonishing collections of stuffed and living birds from all quarters of the world. After I had studied over the latter for a time, I remarked that every species almost that came from distant regions, such as South America, the coast of Guinea, etc., were thick-billed birds of the *loxia* and *fringilla* genera; and no *motacillæ*, or *muscicapæ*, were to be met with. When I came to consider, the reason was obvious enough; for the hard-billed birds subsist on seeds, which are easily carried on board; while the soft-billed birds, which are supported by worms and insects, or, what is a *succedaneum* for them, fresh raw meat, can meet with neither in long and tedious voyages. It is from this defect of food that our collections (curious as they are) are defective, and we are deprived of some of the most delicate and lively genera.

*　　*　　*

I was much pleased to see, among the collection of birds from Gibraltar, some of those short-winged English summer birds of passage, concerning whose departure we have made so much inquiry. Now if these birds are found in Andalusia to migrate to and from Barbary, it may easily be supposed that those that come to us may migrate back to the continent, and spend their winters in some of the warmer parts of Europe. This is certain, that many soft-billed birds that come to Gibraltar appear there only in spring and autumn, seeming to advance in pairs towards the northward, for the sake of breeding during the summer months; and retiring in parties and broods towards the south at the decline of the year: so that the rock of Gibraltar is the great rendezvous, and place of observation, from whence they take their departure each way towards Europe or Africa. It is therefore no mean discovery, I think, to find that our small short-winged summer birds of passage are to be seen spring and autumn on the very skirts of Europe; it is a presumptive proof of their emigrations.

Scopoli seems to me to have found the *hirundo melba*, the great Gibraltar swift, in Tirol, without knowing it. For what is his *hirundo alpina* but the afore-mentioned bird in other words? Says he, '*Omnia prioris*' (meaning the swift); '*sed pectus album; paulo major priore.*' I do not suppose this to be a new species. It is true also of the *melba*, that 'nidificat in excelsis Alpium rupibus.' Vid. Annum Primum.

My Sussex friend, a man of observation and good sense, but no naturalist, to whom I applied on account of the stone curlew, *œdicnemus*, sends me the following account: 'In looking over my Naturalist's Journal for the month of April, I find the stone curlews are first mentioned on the seventeenth and eighteenth, which date seems to me rather late. They live with us all the spring and summer and at the beginning of autumn prepare to take leave by getting together in flocks. They seem to me a bird of passage that may travel into some dry hilly country south of us, probably Spain, because of the abundance of sheep-walks in that country; for they spend their summers with us in such districts. This conjecture I hazard, as I have never met with any one that has seen them in England in the winter. I believe they are not fond of going near the water, but feed on earth-worms, that are common on sheep-walks and downs. They breed on fallows and lay-fields abounding with grey mossy flints, which much resemble their young in colour; among which they skulk and conceal themselves. They make no nest, but lay their eggs on the bare ground, producing in common but two at a time. There is reason to think their young run soon after they are hatched; and that the old ones do not feed them, but only lead them about at the time of feeding, which, for the most part, is in the night.' Thus far my friend.

In the manners of this bird you see there is something very analogous to the bustard, whom it also somewhat resembles in aspect and make, and in the structure of its feet.

For a long time I have desired my relation to look out for these birds in Andalusia; and now he writes me word that, for the first time, he saw one dead in the market on the 3rd of September.

When the *œdicnemus* flies it stretches out its legs straight behind, like an heron.

Letters to Daines Barrington

When I was in town last month I partly engaged that I would sometime do myself the honour to write to you on the subject of natural history: and I am the more ready to fulfil my promise, because I see you are a gentleman of great candour, and one that will make allowances; especially where the writer professes to be an out-door naturalist, one that takes his observations from the subject itself, and not from the writings of others.

The following is a LIST *of the* SUMMER BIRDS *of* PASSAGE *which I have discovered in this neighbourhood, ranged somewhat in the order in which they appear.*

	RAII NOMINA.	USUALLY APPEARS ABOUT
1. Wry-neck,	*Jynx, sive torquilla:*	The middle of March: harsh note.
2. Smallest willow-wren,	*Regulus non cristatus:*	March 23: chirps till September.
3. Swallow,	*Hirundo domestica:*	April 13.
4. Martin,	*Hirundo rustica:*	Ditto.
5. Sand-martin,	*Hirundo riparia:*	Ditto.
6. Black-cap,	*Atricapilla:*	Ditto: a sweet wild note.
7. Nightingale,	*Luscinia:*	Beginning of April.
8. Cuckoo,	*Cuculus:*	Middle of April.
9. Middle willow-wren,	*Regulus non cristatus:*	Ditto, a sweet plaintive note.

	RAII NOMINA.	USUALLY APPEARS ABOUT
10. White-throat,	*Ficedulæ affinis:*	Middle of April: mean note; sings on till September.
11. Red-start,	*Ruticilla:*	Ditto: more agreeable song.
12. Stone curlew,	*Œdicnemus:*	End of March; loud nocturnal whistle.
13. Turtle-dove,	*Turtur:*	
14. Grasshopper-lark,	*Alauda minima locustæ voce*	Middle of April: a small sibilous note, till the end of July.
15. Swift,	*Hirundo apus:*	About April 27.
16. Less reed-sparrow	*Passer arundinaceus minor:*	A sweet polyglot, but hurrying: it has the notes of many birds.
17. Land-rail,	*Ortygometra:*	A loud harsh note, *crex, crex.*
18. Largest willow-wren,	*Regulus non cristatus:*	*Cantat voce stridulá locustæ*; end of April, on the tops of high beeches.
19. Goat-sucker, or fern-owl,	*Caprimulgus:*	Beginning of May; chatters by night with a singular noise.
20. Fly-catcher,	*Stoparola:*	May 12. A very mute bird: this is the latest summer bird of passage.

This assemblage of curious and amusing birds belongs to ten several genera of the Linnæan system; and are all of the *ordo* of *passeres*, save the *jynx* and *cuculus*, which are *picæ*, and the *charadrius* (*œdicnemus*) and *rallus* (*ortygo-metra*) which are *grallæ*.

These birds, as they stand numerically, belong to the following Linnæan genera:

1.	*Jynx.*	13.	*Columba.*
2, 6, 7, 9, 10, 11, 16, 18.	*Motacilla.*	17.	*Rallus.*
3, 4, 5, 15.	*Hirundo.*	19.	*Caprimulgus.*
8.	*Cuculus.*	14.	*Alauda.*
12.	*Charadrius.*	20.	*Muscicapa.*

Most soft-billed birds live on insects, and not on grain and seeds; and therefore at the end of summer they retire: but the following soft-billed birds, though insect-eaters, stay with us the year round:

RAII NOMINA.

Red-breast,	*Rubecula:*	These frequent houses; and haunt outbuildings in the winter; eat spiders.
Wren,	*Paser troglodytes:*	
Hedge-sparrow,	*Curruca:*	Haunt sinks for crumbs and other sweepings.
White-wagtail,	*Motacilla alba:*	These frequent shallow rivulets near the spring heads, where they never freeze: eat the aureliæ of *Phryganea.* The smallest birds that walk.
Yellow-wagtail,	*Motacilla flava:*	
Grey-wagtail,	*Motacilla cinerea:*	
Wheat-ear,	*Œnanthe:*	Some of these are to be seen with us the winter through.

	RAII NOMINA.	
Whin-chat,	*Œnanthe secunda:*	
Stone-chatter,	*Œnanthe tertia:*	
Golden-crowned wren,	*Regulus cristatus:*	This is the smallest British bird: haunts the tops of all trees; stays the winter through.

A LIST *of the* WINTER BIRDS *of* PASSAGE *round this neighbourhood, ranged somewhat in the order in which they appear:*

	RAII NOMINA.	
1. Ring-ousel,	*Merula torquata:*	This is a new migration which I have lately discovered about Michaelmas week, and again about the fourteenth of March.
2. Redwing,	*Turdus iliacus:*	About old Michaelmas.
3. Fieldfare,	*Turdus pilaris:*	Though a percher by day, roosts on the ground.
4. Royston-crow,	*Cornix cinerea:*	Most frequent on downs.
5. Wood-cock,	*Scolopax:*	Appears about old Michaelmas.
6. Snipe,	*Gallinago minor:*	Some snipes constantly breed with us.
7. Jack-snipe,	*Gallinago minima:*	
8. Wood-pigeon,	*Œnas:*	Seldom appears till late: not in such plenty as formerly.
9. Wild-swan,	*Cygnus ferus:*	On some large waters.
10. Wild-goose,	*Anser ferus:*	

	RAII NOMINA.	
11. Wild-duck,	*Anas torquata minor:*	
12. Pochard,	*Anas fera fusca:*	On our streams and lakes.
13. Widgeon,	*Penelope:*	
14. Teal, breeds with us in Wolmer-forest.	*Querquedula:*	
15. Gross-beak,	*Coccothraustes:*	These are only wanderers that appear occasionally, and are not observant of any regular migration.
16. Cross-bill,	*Loxia:*	
17. Silk-tail,	*Garrulus bohemicus:*	

These birds, as they stand numerically, belong to the following Linnæan genera:

1, 2, 3.	*Turdus.*	9, 10, 11, 12, 13, 14.	*Anas.*
4.	*Corvus.*	15, 16.	*Loxia.*
5, 6, 7.	*Scolopax.*	17.	*Ampelis.*
8.	*Columba.*		

Birds that sing in the night are but few:

Nightingale,	*Luscinia:*	'In shadiest covert hid.' – MILTON.
Woodlark,	*Alauda arborea:*	Suspended in mid air.
Less reed-sparrow,	*Passer arundinaceus minor.*	Among reeds and willows.

I should now proceed to such birds as continue to sing after Midsummer, but, as they are rather numerous, they would exceed the bounds of this paper: besides, as this is now the season for remarking on that subject, I am willing to repeat my observations on some birds concerning the continuation of whose song I seem at present to have some doubt.

★   ★   ★

When I did myself the honour to write to you about the end of last June on the subject of natural history, I sent you a list of the summer birds of passage which I have observed in this neighbourhood; and also a list of the winter birds of passage; I mentioned besides those soft-billed birds that stay with us the winter through in the south of England, and those that are remarkable for singing in the night.

According to my proposal, I shall now proceed to such birds (singing birds strictly so called) as continue in full song till after Midsummer; and shall range them somewhat in the order in which they first begin to open as the spring advances.

	RAII NOMINA.	
1. Woodlark,	*Alauda arborea:*	In January, and continues to sing through all the summer and autumn.
2. Song-thrush,	*Turdus simpliciter dictus:*	In February and on to August, reassume their song in autumn.
3. Wren,	*Passer troglodytes:*	All the year, hard frost excepted.
4. Red-breast,	*Rubecula:*	Ditto.
5. Hedge-sparrow,	*Curruca:*	Early in February to July the 10th.

RAII NOMINA.

6. Yellow-hammer,	*Emberiza flava:*	Early in February, and on through July to August the 21st.
7. Skylark,	*Alauda vulgaris:*	In February, and on to October.
8. Swallow,	*Hirundo domestica:*	From April to September.
9. Black-cap,	*Atricapilla:*	Beginning of April to July 13th.
10. Titlark,	*Alauda pratorum:*	From middle of April to July the 16th.
11. Blackbird,	*Merula vulgaris:*	Sometimes in February and March, and so on to July the twenty-third; reassumes in autumn.
12. White-throat,	*Ficedulæ affinis:*	In April and on to July 23.
13. Goldfinch,	*Carduelis:*	April and through to September 16.
14. Greenfinch,	*Chloris:*	On to July and August 2.
15. Less reed-sparrow,	*Passer arundinaceus minor:*	May, on to beginning of July.
16. Common linnet,	*Linaria vulgaris:*	Breeds and whistles on till August; reassumes its note when they begin to congregate in October, and again early before the flock separate.

Birds that cease to be in full song, and are usually silent at or before Midsummer:

RAII NOMINA.

17. Middle willow-wren,	*Regulus non cristatus:*	Middle of June: begins in April.
18. Red-start,	*Ruticilla:*	Middle of June: begins in May.
19. Chaffinch,	*Fringilla:*	Beginning of June:sings first in February.
20. Nightingale,	*Luscinia:*	Middle of June: sings first in April.

Birds that sing for a short time, and very early in the spring:

21. Missel-bird,	*Turdus viscivorus:*	January the 2nd, 1770, in February. Is called in Hampshire and Sussex the storm-cock, because its song is supposed to forebode windy wet weather: is the largest singing bird we have.
22. Great tit-mouse, or ox-eye,	*Fringillago:*	In February, March, April: reassumes for a short time in September.

Birds that have somewhat of a note or song, and yet are hardly to be called singing birds:

23. Golden-crowned wren,	*Regulus cristatus:*	Its note as minute as its person; frequents the tops of high oaks and firs; the smallest British bird.

RAII NOMINA.

24. Marsh titmouse	*Parus palustris:*	Haunts great woods; two harsh sharp notes.
25. Small willow-wren,	*Regulus non cristatus:*	Sings in March and on to September.
26. Largest ditto,	*Ditto:*	*Cantat voce stridulâ locustæ:* from end of April to August.
27. Grasshopper-lark,	*Alauda minima voce locustæ:*	Chirps all night, from the middle of April to the end of July.
28. Martin,	*Hirundo agrestis:*	All the breeding time; from May to September.
29. Bullfinch,	*Pyrrhula:*	
30. Bunting,	*Emberiza alba:*	From the end of January to July.

All singing birds, and those that have any pretensions to song, not only in Britain, but perhaps the world through, come under the Linnæan *ordo* of *passeres*.

The above-mentioned birds, as they stand numerically, belong to the following Linnæan genera.

1, 7, 10, 27.	*Alauda.*	8, 28.	*Hirundo.*
2, 11, 21.	*Turdus.*	13, 16, 19.	*Fringilla.*
3, 4, 5, 9, 12, 15, 17, 18, 20, 23, 25, 26. }	*Motacilla.*	22, 24.	*Parus.*
6, 30.	*Emberiza.*	14, 29.	*Loxia.*

Birds that sing as they fly are but few:

RAII NOMINA.

Skylark,	*Alauda vulgaris:*	Rising, suspended, and falling.
Titlark,	*Alauda pratorum:*	In its descent; also sitting on trees, and walking on the ground.
Woodlark,	*Alauda arborea:*	Suspended; in hot summer nights all night long.
Blackbird,	*Merula:*	Sometimes from bush to bush.
White-throat,	*Ficedulæ affinis:*	Uses when singing on the wing odd jerks and gesticulations.
Swallow,	*Hirundo domestica:*	In soft sunny weather.
Wren,	*Passer troglodytes:*	Sometimes from bush to bush.

Birds that breed most early in these parts:

Raven,	*Corvus:*	Hatches in February and March.
Song-thrush,	*Turdus:*	In March.
Blackbird,	*Merula:*	In March.

Rook,	*Cornix frugilega:*	Builds the beginning of March.
Woodlark,	*Alauda arborea:*	Hatches in April.
Ring-dove,	*Palumbus torquatus:*	Lays the beginning of April.

All birds that continue in full song till after Midsummer appear to me to breed more than once.

Most kinds of birds seem to me to be wild and shy somewhat in proportion to their bulk; I mean in this island, where they are much pursued and annoyed: but in Ascension-island, and many other desolate places, mariners have found fowls so unacquainted with an human figure, that they would stand still to be taken; as is the case with boobies, etc. As an example of what is advanced, I remark that the golden-crested wren (the smallest British bird) will stand unconcerned till you come within three or four yards of it, while the bustard (*otis*), the largest British land fowl, does not care to admit a person within so many furlongs.

*   *   *

It was no small matter of satisfaction to me to find that you were not displeased with my little *methodus* of birds. If there was any merit in the sketch, it must be owing to its punctuality. For many months I carried a list in my pocket of the birds that were to be remarked, and, as I rode or walked about my business, I noted each day the continuance or omission of each bird's song; so that I am as sure of the certainty of my facts as a man can be of any transaction whatsoever.

I shall now proceed to answer the several queries which you put in your two obliging letters, in the best manner that I am able. Perhaps Eastwick, and its environs, where you heard so very few birds, is not a woodland country, and therefore not stocked with such songsters. If you will cast your eye on my last letter, you will find that many species continued to warble after the beginning of July.

The titlark and yellow-hammer breed late, the latter very late; and therefore it is no wonder that they protract their song; for I lay it down as a maxim in ornithology, that as long as there is any incubation going on there is music. As to the red-breast and wren, it is well known to the most incurious observer that they whistle the year round, hard frost excepted; especially the latter.

It was not in my power to procure you a black-cap, or a less reed-sparrow, or sedge-bird, alive. As the first is undoubtedly, and the last, as far as I can see yet, a summer bird of passage, they would require more nice and curious management in a cage than I should be able to give them; they are both distinguished songsters. The note of the former has such a wild sweetness that it always brings to my mind those lines in a song in *As You Like It*,

> And tune his merry note
> Unto the *wild* bird's throat.

> Shakespeare.

The latter has a surprising variety of notes resembling the song of several other birds; but then it also has an hurrying manner, not at all to its advantage; it is notwithstanding a delicate polyglot.

It is new to me that titlarks in cages sing in the night; perhaps only caged birds do so. I once knew a tame red-breast in a cage that always sang as long as candles were in the room; but in their wild state no one supposes they sing in the night.

I should be almost ready to doubt the fact, that there are to be seen much fewer birds in July than in any former month, notwithstanding so many young are hatched daily. Sure I am that it is far otherwise with respect to the swallow tribe, which increases prodigiously as the summer advances: and I saw, at the time mentioned, many hundreds of young wagtails on the banks of the Cherwell, which almost covered the meadows. If the matter appears as you say in the other species, may it not be owing to the dams being engaged in incubation, while the young are concealed by the leaves?

Many times have I had the curiosity to open the stomachs of woodcocks and snipes; but nothing ever occurred that helped to explain to me what their subsistence might be: all that I could ever find was a soft mucus, among which lay many pellucid small gravels.

*　　*　　*

Your observation that 'the cuckoo does not deposit its egg indiscriminately in the nest of the first bird that comes in its way, but probably looks out a nurse in some degree congenerous, with whom to intrust its young,' is perfectly new to me; and struck me so forcibly, that

I naturally fell into a train of thought that led me to consider whether the fact was so, and what reason there was for it. When I came to recollect and inquire, I could not find that any cuckoo had ever been seen in these parts, except in the nest of the wagtail, the hedge-sparrow, the titlark, the white-throat, and the red-breast, all soft-billed insectivorous birds. The excellent Mr Willughby mentions the nest of the *palumbus* (ring-dove), and of the *fringilla* (chaffinch), birds that subsist on acorns and grains, and such hard food: but then he does not mention them as of his own knowledge: but says afterwards that he saw himself a wagtail feeding a cuckoo. It appears hardly possible that a soft-billed bird should subsist on the same food with the hard-billed: for the former have thin membranaceous stomachs suited to their soft food; while the latter, the granivorous tribe, have strong muscular gizzards, which, like mills, grind, by the help of small gravels and pebbles what is swallowed. This proceeding of the cuckoo, of dropping its eggs as it were by chance, is such a monstrous outrage on maternal affection, one of the first great dictates of nature, and such a violence on instinct, that, had it only been related of a bird in the Brazils, or Peru, it would never have merited our belief. But yet, should it farther appear that this simple bird, when divested of the natural στοργὴ that seems to raise the kind in general above themselves, and inspire them with extraordinary degrees of cunning and address, may be still endued with a more enlarged faculty of discerning what species are suitable and congenerous nursing-mothers for its disregarded eggs and young, and may deposit them only under their care, this would be adding wonder to wonder, and instancing in a fresh manner that the methods of Providence are not subjected to any mode or rule, but astonish us in new lights, and in various and changeable appearances.

What was said by a very ancient and sublime writer concerning the defect of natural affection in the ostrich, may be well applied to the bird we are talking of:

'She is hardened against her young ones, as though they were not hers:

Because God hath deprived her of wisdom, neither hath he imparted to her understanding.'

Query. – Does each female cuckoo lay but one egg in a season, or does she drop several in different nests according as opportunity offers?

* * *

You are, I know, no great friend to migration; and the well attested accounts from various parts of the kingdom seem to justify you in your suspicions, that at least many of the swallow kind do not leave us in the winter, but lay themselves up like insects and bats, in a torpid state, to slumber away the more uncomfortable months till the return of the sun and fine weather awakens them.

But then we must not, I think, deny migration in general; because migration certainly does subsist in some places, as my brother in Andalusia has fully informed me. Of the motions of these birds he has ocular demonstration for many weeks together, both spring and fall:

during which periods myriads of the swallow kind traverse the Straits from north to south, and from south to north, according to the season. And these vast migrations consist not only of *hirundines* but of bee-birds, hoopoes, *oro pendolos* or golden thrushes, etc., etc., and also many of our soft-billed summer-birds of passage; and moreover of birds which never leave us, such as all the various sorts of hawks and kites. Old Belon, two hundred years ago, gives a curious account of the incredible armies of hawks and kites which he saw in the spring-time traversing the Thracian Bosphorus from Asia to Europe. Besides the above-mentioned, he remarks that the procession is swelled by whole troops of eagles and vultures.

Now it is no wonder that birds residing in Africa should retreat before the sun as it advances, and retire to milder regions, and especially birds of prey, whose blood being heated with hot animal food, are more impatient of a sultry climate: but then I cannot help wondering why kites and hawks, and such hardy birds as are known to defy all the severity of England, and even of Sweden and all north Europe, should want to migrate from the south of Europe, and be dissatisfied with the winters of Andalusia.

It does not appear to me that much stress may be laid on the difficulty and hazard that birds must run in their migrations, by reason of vast oceans, cross winds, etc.; because, if we reflect, a bird may travel from England to the equator without launching out and exposing itself to boundless seas, and that by crossing the water at Dover, and again at Gibraltar. And I with the more confidence advance this obvious remark, because my brother has always found that some of his birds, and particularly the swallow kind, are very sparing of their pains in crossing the Mediterranean: for when arrived at Gibraltar, they do not

> . . . rang'd in figure wedge their way,
> . . . and set forth
> Their airy caravan high over seas
> Flying, and over lands with mutual wing
> Easing their flight . . .
>
> Milton.

but scout and hurry along in little detached parties of six or seven in a company; and sweeping low, just over the surface of the land and water, direct their course to the opposite continent at the narrowest passage they can find. They usually slope across the bay to the south-west, and so pass over opposite to Tangier, which, it seems, is the narrowest space.

In former letters we have considered whether it was probable that woodcocks in moon-shiny nights cross the German ocean from Scandinavia. As a proof that birds of less speed may pass that sea, considerable as it is, I shall relate the following incident, which, though mentioned to have happened so many years ago, was strictly matter of fact: As some people were shooting in the parish of Trotton, in the county of Sussex, they killed a duck in that dreadful winter 1708–9, with a silver collar about its neck, on which were engraven the arms of the king of Denmark. This anecdote the rector of Trotton at that time has often told to a near relation of mine;

and, to the best of my remembrance, the collar was in the possession of the rector.

At present I do not know anybody near the sea-side that will take the trouble to remark at what time of the moon woodcocks first come: if I lived near the sea myself I would soon tell you more of the matter. One thing I used to observe when I was a sportsman, that there were times in which woodcocks were so sluggish and sleepy that they would drop again when flushed just before the spaniels, nay, just at the muzzle of a gun that had been fired at them: whether this strange laziness was the effect of a recent fatiguing journey I shall not presume to say.

Nightingales not only never reach Northumberland and Scotland, but also, as I have been always told, Devonshire and Cornwall. In those two last counties we cannot attribute the failure of them to the want of warmth: the defect in the west is rather a presumptive argument that these birds come over to us from the continent at the narrowest passage, and do not stroll so far westward.

Let me hear from your own observation whether skylarks do not dust. I think they do: and if they do, whether they wash also.

The *alauda pratensis* of Ray was the poor dupe that was educating the booby of a cuckoo mentioned in my letter of October last.

Your letter came too late for me to procure a ring-ousel for Mr Tunstal during their autumnal visit; but I will endeavour to get him one when they call on us again in April. I am glad that you and that gentleman saw my Andalusian birds; I hope they answered your expectation. Royston, or grey crows, are winter birds that come much about the same time with the wood-cock: they, like the fieldfare and redwing, have no apparent reason for migration; for as they fare in the winter like their congeners, so might they in all appearance in the summer. Was not Tenant, when a boy, mistaken? did he not find a missel-thrush's nest, and take it for the nest of a fieldfare?

The stock-dove, or wood-pigeon, *œnas Raii*, is the last winter bird of passage which appears with us; and is not seen till towards the end of November: about twenty years ago they abounded in the district of Selborne; and strings of them were seen morning and evening that reached a mile or more: but since the beechen woods have been greatly thinned they are much decreased in number. The ring-dove, *palumbus Raii*, stays with us the whole year, and breeds several times through the summer.

Before I received your letter of October last I had just remarked in my journal that the trees were unusually green. This uncommon verdure lasted on late into November; and may be accounted for from a late spring, a cool and moist summer; but more particularly from vast armies of chafers, or tree beetles, which, in many places, reduced whole woods to a leafless naked state. These trees shot again at Midsummer, and then retained their foliage till very late in the year.

My musical friend, at whose house I am now visiting, has tried all the owls that are his near neighbours with a pitch-pipe, set at concert-pitch, and finds they all hoot in B flat. He will examine the nightingales next spring.

*   *   *

From what follows, it will appear that neither owls nor cuckoos keep to one note. A friend remarks that many (most) of his owls hoot in B flat: but that one went almost half a note below A. The pipe he tried their notes by was a common half-crown pitch-pipe, such as masters use for tuning of harpsichords; it was the common London pitch.

A neighbour of mine, who is said to have a nice ear, remarks that the owls about this village hoot in three different keys, in G flat, or F sharp, in B flat and A flat. He heard two hooting to each other, the one in A flat, and the other in B flat. *Query:* Do these different notes proceed from different species, or only from various individuals? The same person finds upon trial that the note of the cuckoo (of which we have but one species) varies in different individuals; for, about Selborne wood, he found they were mostly in D: he heard two sing together, the one in D, the other in D sharp, who made a disagreeable concert: he afterwards heard one in D sharp, and about Wolmer-forest some in C. As to nightingales, he says that their notes are so short, and their transitions so rapid, that he cannot well ascertain their key. Perhaps in a cage, and in a room, their notes may be more distinguishable. This person has tried to settle the notes of a swift, and of several other small birds, but cannot bring them to any criterion.

As I have often remarked that redwings are some of the first birds that suffer with us in severe weather, it is no wonder at all that they retreat from Scandinavian winters: and much more the *ordo* of *grallæ*, who, all to a bird, forsake the northern parts of Europe at the approach of winter. *'Grallæ tanquam conjuratæ unanimiter in fugam se conjiciunt; ne earum unicam quidem inter nos habitantem invenire possimus; ut enim æstate in australibus degere nequeunt ob defectum lumbricorum, terramque siccam; ita nec in frigidis ob eandem causam,'* says Eckmarck the Swede, in his ingenious little treatise called *Migrationes Avium*, which by all means you ought to read while your thoughts run on the subject of migration. See *Amœnitates Academicæ*, vol. iv, p. 565.

Birds may be so circumstanced as to be obliged to migrate in one country and not in another: but the *grallæ* (which procure their food from marshes and boggy grounds) must in winter forsake the more northerly parts of Europe, or perish for want of food.

I am glad you are making inquiries from Linnæus concerning the woodcock: it is expected of him that he should be able to account for the motions and manner of life of the animals of his own *Fauna*.

Faunists, as you observe, are too apt to acquiesce in bare descriptions, and a few synonyms: the reason is plain; because all that may be done at home in a man's study, but the investigation of the life and conversation of animals, is a concern of much more trouble and difficulty, and is not to be attained but by the active and inquisitive, and by those that reside much in the country.

Foreign systematics are, I observe, much too vague in their specific differences; which are almost universally constituted by one or two particular marks, the rest of the description running in general terms. But our countryman, the excellent Mr Ray, is the only describer that conveys some precise idea in every term or word, maintaining his superiority over his followers and imitators in spite of the advantage of fresh discoveries and modern information.

At this distance of years it is not in my power to recollect at what periods woodcocks used to be sluggish or alert when I was a sportsman; but, upon my mentioning this circumstance to a friend, he thinks he has observed them to be remarkably listless against snowy foul weather: if this should be the case, then the inaptitude for flying arises only from an eagerness for food; as sheep are observed to be very intent on grazing against stormy wet evenings.

* * *

While I was in Sussex last autumn my residence was at the village near Lewes, from whence I had formerly the pleasure of writing to you. On the first of November I remarked that the old tortoise, formerly mentioned, began first to dig the ground in order to the forming its hybernaculum, which it had fixed on just beside a great tuft of hepaticas. It scrapes out the ground with its fore-feet, and throws it up over its back with its hind; but the motion of its legs is ridiculously slow, little exceeding the hour-hand of a clock; and suitable to the composure of an animal said to be a whole month in performing one feat of copulation. Nothing can be more assiduous than this creature night and day in scooping the earth, and forcing its great body into the cavity; but, as the noons of that season proved unusually warm and sunny, it was continually interrupted, and called forth by the heat in the middle of the day; and though I continued there till the thirteenth of November, yet the work remained unfinished. Harsher weather, and frosty mornings, would have quickened its operations. No part of its behaviour ever struck me more than the extreme timidity it always expresses with regard to rain; for though it has a shell that would secure it against the wheel of a loaded cart, yet does it discover as much solicitude about rain as a lady dressed in all her best attire, shuffling away on the first sprinklings, and running its head up in a corner. If attended to, it becomes an excellent weather-glass; for as sure as it walks elate, and as it were on tiptoe, feeding with great earnestness in a morning, so sure will it rain before night. It is totally a diurnal animal, and never pretends to stir after it becomes dark. The tortoise, like other reptiles, has an arbitrary stomach as well as lungs; and can refrain from eating as well as breathing for a great part of the year. When first awakened it eats nothing; nor again in the autumn before it retires: through the height of the summer it feeds voraciously, devouring all the food that comes in its way. I was much taken with its sagacity in discerning those that do it kind offices; for, as soon as the good old lady comes in sight who has waited on it for more than thirty years, it hobbles towards its benefactress with awkward alacrity; but remains inattentive to strangers. Thus not only '*the ox knoweth his owner, and the ass his master's crib,*' but the most abject reptile and torpid of beings distinguishes the hand that feeds it, and is touched with the feelings of gratitude!

P.S. In about three days after I left Sussex the tortoise retired into the ground under the hepatica.

* * *

The more I reflect on the στοργή of animals, the more I am astonished at its effects. Nor is the violence of this affection more wonderful than the shortness of its duration. Thus every hen is in her turn the virago of the yard, in proportion to the helplessness of her brood; and will fly in the face of a dog or a sow in defence of those chickens, which in a few weeks she will drive before her with relentless cruelty.

This affection sublimes the passions, quickens the invention, and sharpens the sagacity of the brute creation. Thus an hen, just become a mother, is no longer that placid bird she used to be, but with feathers standing on end, wings hovering, and clocking note, she runs about like one possessed. Dams will throw themselves in the way of the greatest danger in order to avert it from their progeny. Thus a partridge will tumble along before a sportsman in order to draw away the dogs from her helpless covey. In the time of nidification the most feeble birds will assault the most rapacious. All the *hirundines* of a village are up in arms at the sight of an hawk, whom they will persecute till he leaves that district. A very exact observer has often remarked that a pair of ravens nesting in the rock of Gibraltar would suffer no vulture or eagle to rest near their station, but would drive them from the hill with an amazing fury: even the blue thrush at the season of breeding would dart out from the clefts of the rocks to chase away the kestril, or the sparrow-hawk. If you stand near the nest of a bird that has young, she will not be induced to betray them by an inadvertent fondness, but will wait about at a distance with meat in her mouth for an hour together.

Should I farther corroborate what I have advanced above by some anecdotes which I probably may have mentioned before in conversation, yet you will, I trust, pardon the repetition for the sake of illustration.

The fly-catcher of the *Zoology* (the *stoparola* of Ray), builds every year in the vines that grow on the walls of my house. A pair of these little birds had one year inadvertently placed their nest on a naked bough, perhaps in a shady time; not being aware of the inconvenience that followed. But an hot sunny season coming on before the brood was half fledged, the reflection of the wall became insupportable, and must inevitably have destroyed the tender young, had not affection suggested an expedient, and prompted the parent-birds to hover over the nest all the hotter hours, while with wings expanded, and mouths gaping for breath, they screened off the heat from their suffering offspring.

A farther instance I once saw of notable sagacity in a willow-wren, which had built in a bank in my fields. This bird a friend and myself had observed as she sat in her nest; but were particularly careful not to disturb her, though we saw she eyed us with some degree of jealousy. Some days after as we passed that way we were desirous of remarking how this brood went on; but no nest could be found, till I happened to take up a large bundle of long green moss, as it were, carelessly thrown over the nest, in order to dodge the eye of any impertinent intruder.

A still more remarkable mixture of sagacity and instinct occurred to me one day as my people were pulling off the lining of an hotbed, in order to add some fresh dung. From out of the side of this bed leaped an animal with great agility that made a most grotesque figure; nor was it without great difficulty that it could be taken; when it proved to be a large white-bellied field-mouse with three or four young clinging to her teats by their mouths and feet. It was amazing that the desultory and rapid motions of this dam should not oblige her litter to quit their hold, especially when it appeared that they were so young as to be both naked and blind!

To these instances of tender attachment, many more of which might be daily discovered by those that are studious of nature, may be opposed that rage of affection, that monstrous perversion of the στοργή, which induces some females of the brute creation to devour their young because their owners have handled them too freely, or removed them from place to place! Swine, and sometimes the more gentle race of dogs and cats, are guilty of this horrid and preposterous murder. When I hear now and then of an abandoned mother that destroys her offspring, I am not so much amazed; since reason perverted, and the bad passions let loose, are capable of any enormity: but why the parental feelings of brutes, that usually flow in one most uniform tenor, should sometimes be so extravagantly diverted, I leave to abler philosophers than myself to determine.

*   *   *

Some young men went down lately to a pond on the verge of Wolmer-forest to hunt flappers, or young wild-ducks, many of which they caught, and, among the rest, some very minute yet well-fledged wild-fowls alive, which, upon examination, I found to be teals. I did not know till then that teals ever bred in the south of England, and was much pleased with the discovery: this I look upon as a great stroke in natural history.

We have had, ever since I can remember, a pair of white owls that constantly breed under the eaves of this church. As I have paid good attention to the manner of life of these birds during their season of breeding, which lasts the summer through, the following remarks may not perhaps be unacceptable: About an hour before sunset (for then the mice begin to run) they sally forth in quest of prey, and hunt all round the hedges of meadows and small enclosures for them, which seem to be their only food. In this irregular country we can stand on an eminence and see them beat the fields over like a setting-dog, and often drop down in the grass or corn. I have minuted these birds with my watch for an hour together, and have found that they return to their nests, the one or the other of them, about once in five minutes; reflecting at the same time on the adroitness that every animal is possessed of as regards the well-being of itself and offspring. But a piece of address, which they show when they return loaded, should not, I think, be passed over in silence. – As they take their prey with their claws, so they carry it in their claws to their nest: but, as the feet are necessary in their ascent under the tiles, they constantly perch first on the roof of the chancel, and shift the mouse from their claws to their bill, that the feet may be at liberty to take hold of the plate on the wall as they are rising under the eaves.

White owls seem not (but in this I am not positive) to

hoot at all: all that clamorous hooting appears to me to come from the wood kinds. The white owl does indeed snore and hiss in a tremendous manner; and these menaces will answer the intention of intimidating: for I have known a whole village up in arms on such an occasion, imagining the church-yard to be full of goblins and spectres. White owls also often scream horribly as they fly along; from this screaming probably arose the common people's imaginary species of screech-owl, which they superstitiously think attends the windows of dying persons. The plumage of the remiges of the wings of every species of owl that I have yet examined is remarkably soft and pliant. Perhaps it may be necessary that the wings of these birds should not make much resistance or rushing, that they may be enabled to steal through the air unheard upon a nimble and watchful quarry.

While I am talking of owls, it may not be improper to mention what I was told by a gentleman of the county of Wilts. As they were grubbing a vast hollow pollard-ash that had been the mansion of owls for centuries, he discovered at the bottom a mass of matter that at first he could not account for. After some examination, he found it was a congeries of the bones of mice (and perhaps of birds and bats) that had been heaping together for ages, being cast up in pellets out of the crops of many generations of inhabitants. For owls cast up the bones, fur and feathers of what they devour, after the manner of hawks. He believes, he told me, that there were bushels of this kind of substance.

When brown owls hoot their throats swell as big as

an hen's egg. I have known an owl of this species live a full year without any water. Perhaps the case may be the same with all birds of prey. When owls fly they stretch out their legs behind them as a balance to their large heavy heads; for as most nocturnal birds have large eyes and ears they must have large heads to contain them. Large eyes I presume are necessary to collect every ray of light, and large concave ears to command the smallest degree of sound or noise.

*   *   *

By means of a straight cottage chimney I had an opportunity this summer of remarking, at my leisure, how swallows ascend and descend through the shaft; but my pleasure, in contemplating the address with which this feat was performed to a considerable depth in the chimney, was somewhat interrupted by apprehensions lest my eyes might undergo the same fate with those of Tobit.

Perhaps it may be some amusement to you to hear at what times the different species of *hirundines* arrived this spring in three very distant counties of this kingdom. With us the swallow was seen first on April the 4th, the swift on April the 24th, the bank-martin on April the 12th, and the house-martin not till April the 30th. At South Zele, Devonshire, swallows did not arrive till April the 25th; swifts, in plenty, on May the 1st; and house-martins not till the middle of May. At Blackburn, in Lancashire, swifts were seen April the 28th, swallows April the 29th, house-martins May the 1st. Do these different dates, in such distant districts, prove anything for or against migration?

A farmer, near Weyhill, fallows his land with two teams of asses; one of which works till noon, and the other in the afternoon. When these animals have done their work, they are penned, all night, like sheep, on the fallow. In the winter they are confined and foddered in a yard, and make plenty of dung.

Linnæus says that hawks '*paciscuntur inducias cum avibus, quamdiu cuculus cuculat*': but it appears to me that, during that period, many little birds are taken and destroyed by birds of prey, as may be seen by their feathers left in lanes and under hedges.

The missel-thrush is, while breeding, fierce and pugnacious, driving such birds as approach its nest, with great fury, to a distance. The Welch call it *pen y llwyn*, the head or master of the coppice. He suffers no magpie, jay, or blackbird, to enter the garden where he haunts; and is, for the time, a good guard to the new-sown legumens. In general he is very successful in the defence of his family: but once I observed in my garden, that several magpies came determined to storm the nest of a missel-thrush: the dams defended their mansion with great vigour, and fought resolutely *pro aris & focis*; but numbers at last prevailed, they tore the nest to pieces, and swallowed the young alive.

In the season of nidification the wildest birds are comparatively tame. Thus the ring-dove breeds in my fields, though they are continually frequented; and the missel-thrush, though most shy and wild in the autumn and winter, builds in my garden close to a walk where people are passing all day long.

Wall-fruit abounds with me this year: but my grapes,

that used to be forward and good, are at present backward beyond all precedent: and this is not the worst of the story; for the same ungenial weather, the same black cold solstice, has injured the more necessary fruits of the earth, and discoloured and blighted our wheat. The crop of hops promises to be very large.

Frequent returns of deafness incommode me sadly, and half disqualify me for a naturalist; for, when those fits are upon me, I lose all the pleasing notices and little intimations arising from rural sounds: and May is to me as silent and mute with respect to the notes of birds, etc., as August. My eyesight is, thank God, quick and good; but with respect to the other sense, I am, at times, disabled:

And Wisdom at one entrance quite shut out.

*   *   *

On September the 21st, 1741, being then on a visit, and intent on field-diversions, I rose before daybreak: when I came into the enclosures, I found the stubbles and clover-grounds matted all over with a thick coat of cobweb, in the meshes of which a copious and heavy dew hung so plentifully that the whole face of the country seemed, as it were, covered with two or three setting-nets drawn one over another. When the dogs attempted to hunt, their eyes were so blinded and hoodwinked that they could not proceed, but were obliged to lie down and scrape the incumbrances from their faces with their fore-feet, so that, finding my sport interrupted, I returned home musing in my mind on the oddness of the occurrence.

As the morning advanced the sun became bright and warm, and the day turned out one of those most lovely ones which no season but the autumn produces: cloudless, calm, serene, and worthy of the South of France itself.

About nine an appearance very unusual began to demand our attention, a shower of cobwebs falling from very elevated regions, and continuing, without any interruption, till the close of the day. These webs were not single filmy threads, floating in the air in all directions, but perfect flakes or rags; some near an inch broad, and five or six long, which fell with a degree of velocity which showed they were considerably heavier than the atmosphere.

On every side as the observer turned his eyes might he behold a continual succession of fresh flakes falling into his sight, and twinkling like stars as they turned their sides towards the sun.

How far this wonderful shower extended would be difficult to say; but we know that it reached Bradley, Selborne, and Alresford, three places which lie in a sort of a triangle, the shortest of whose sides is about eight miles in extent.

At the second of those places there was a gentleman (for whose veracity and intelligent turn we have the greatest veneration) who observed it the moment he got abroad; but concluded that, as soon as he came upon the hill above his house, where he took his morning rides, he should be higher than this meteor, which he imagined might have been blown, like thistle-down, from the common above: but, to his great astonishment, when he rode to the most elevated part of the down, 300 feet above his fields, he found the webs in appearance still as much above him as before; still descending into sight in a constant succession, and twinkling in the sun, so as to draw the attention of the most incurious.

Neither before nor after was any such fall observed; but on this day the flakes hung in the trees and hedges so thick, that a diligent person sent out might have gathered baskets full.

The remark that I shall make on these cobweb-like appearances, called gossamer, is, that, strange and superstitious as the notions about them were formerly, nobody in these days doubts but that they are the real production of small spiders, which swarm in the fields in fine weather in autumn, and have a power of shooting out webs from their tails so as to render themselves buoyant, and lighter than air. But why these apterous insects should that day take such a wonderful aerial excursion, and why their webs should at once become so gross and material as to be considerably more weighty than air, and to descend with precipitation, is a matter beyond my skill. If I might be allowed to hazard a supposition, I should imagine that those filmy threads, when first shot, might be entangled in the rising dew, and so drawn up, spiders and all, by a brisk evaporation into the region where clouds are formed: and if the spiders have a power of coiling and thickening their webs in the air, as Dr Lister says they have, then, when they were become heavier than the air, they must fall.

Every day in fine weather, in autumn chiefly, do I see those spiders shooting out their webs and mounting aloft: they will go off from your finger if you will take them into your hand. Last summer one alighted on my book as I was reading in the parlour; and, running to the top of the page, and shooting out a web, took its departure from thence. But what I most wondered at, was that it went off with considerable velocity in a place where no air was stirring; and I am sure that I did not assist it with my breath. So that these little crawlers seem to have while mounting, some loco-motive power without the use of wings, and to move in the air, faster than the air itself.

*   *   *

There is a wonderful spirit of sociality in the brute creation, independent of sexual attachment: the congregating of gregarious birds in the winter is a remarkable instance.

Many horses, though quiet with company, will not stay one minute in a field by themselves: the strongest fences cannot restrain them. My neighbour's horse will not only not stay by himself abroad, but he will not bear to be left alone in a strange stable without discovering the utmost impatience, and endeavouring to break the rack and manger with his fore feet. He has been known to leap out at a stable-window, through which dung was thrown, after company; and yet in other respects is remarkably quiet. Oxen and cows will not fatten by themselves but will neglect the finest pasture that is not recommended by society. If would be needless to instance in sheep, which constantly flock together.

But this propensity seems not to be confined to animals of the same species; for we know a doe still alive, that was brought up from a little fawn with a dairy of cows; with them it goes afield, and with them it returns to the yard. The dogs of the house take no notice of this deer, being used to her; but, if strange dogs come by, a chase ensues; while the master smiles to see his favourite securely leading her pursuers over hedge, or gate, or stile, till she returns to the cows, who, with fierce lowings and menacing horns, drive the assailants quite out of the pasture.

Even great disparity of kind and size does not always prevent social advances and mutual fellowship. For a very intelligent and observant person has assured me that, in the former part of his life, keeping but one horse, he happened also on a time to have but one solitary hen. These two incongruous animals spent much of their time together in a lonely orchard, where they saw no creature but each other. By degrees an apparent regard began to take place between these two sequestered individuals. The fowl would approach the quadruped with notes of complacency, rubbing herself gently against his legs; while the horse would look down with satisfaction, and move with the greatest caution and circumspection, lest he should trample on his diminutive companion. Thus, by mutual good offices, each seemed to console the vacant hours of the other: so that Milton, when he puts the following sentiment in the mouth of Adam, seems to be somewhat mistaken:

> Much less can bird with beast, or fish with fowl,
> So well converse, nor with the ox the ape.

*   *   *

A good ornithologist should be able to distinguish birds by their air as well as by their colours and shape; on the ground as well as on the wind, and in the bush as well as in the hand. For, though it must not be said that every species of birds has a manner peculiar to itself, yet there is somewhat in most genera at least, that at first sight discriminates them, and enables a judicious observer to pronounce upon them with some certainty. Put a bird in motion.

. . . *Et verâ incessu patuit.* . . .

Thus kites and buzzards sail round in circles with wings expanded and motionless; and it is from their gliding manner that the former are still called in the north of England gleads, from the Saxon verb *glidan* to glide. The kestrel, or wind-hover, has a peculiar mode of hanging in the air in one place, his wings all the while being briskly agitated. Hen-carriers fly low over heaths or fields of corn, and beat the ground regularly like a pointer or setting-dog. Owls move in a buoyant manner, as if lighter than the air; they seem to want ballast. There is a peculiarity belonging to ravens that must draw the attention even of the most incurious – they spend all their leisure time in striking and cuffing each other on the wing in a kind of playful skirmish; and, when they move from one place to another, frequently turn on their backs with a loud croak, and seem to be falling to the ground. When this odd gesture betides them, they are scratching themselves with one foot, and thus lose the centre of gravity. Rooks sometimes dive and tumble in a frolicsome manner; crows and daws swagger in their walk; wood-peckers fly *volatu undoso*, opening and closing their wings at every stroke, and so are always rising or falling in curves. All of this genus use their tails, which incline downward, as a support while they run up trees. Parrots, like all other hook-clawed birds, walk awkwardly, and make use of their bill as a third foot, climbing and ascending with ridiculous caution. All the *gallinæ* parade and walk gracefully, and run nimbly; but fly with difficulty, with an impetuous whirring, and in a straight line. Magpies and jays flutter with powerless wings, and make no dispatch; herons seem incumbered with too much sail for their light bodies; but these vast hollow wings are necessary in carrying burdens, such as large fishes, and the like; pigeons, and particularly the sort called smiters, have a way of clashing their wings the one against the other over their backs with a loud snap; another variety called tumblers turn themselves over in the air. Some birds have movements peculiar to the season of love: thus ring-doves, though strong and rapid at other times, yet in the spring hang about on the wing in a toying and playful manner; thus the cock-snipe, while breeding, forgetting his former flight, fans the air like the wind-hover; and the green-finch in particular exhibits such languishing and faltering gestures as to appear like a wounded and dying bird; the king-fisher darts along like an arrow; fern-owls, or goat-suckers, glance in the dusk over the tops of trees like a meteor; starlings as it were swim along, while missel-thrushes use a wild and desultory flight; swallows sweep over the surface of the ground and water, and distinguish themselves by rapid turns and quick evolutions; swifts dash round in circles; and the bank-martin moves with frequent vacillations like a butterfly. Most of the small birds fly by jerks, rising and falling as they advance. Most small birds hop; but wagtails and larks walk, moving their legs alternately. Skylarks rise and fall perpendicularly as they sing: woodlarks hang poised in the air; and titlarks rise and fall in large curves, singing in their descent. The white-throat uses odd jerks and gesticulations over the tops of hedges and bushes. All the duck-kind waddle; divers and auks walk as if fettered, and stand erect on their tails: these are the *compedes* of Linnæus. Geese and cranes, and most wild-fowls, move in figured flights, often changing their position. The secondary remiges of *tringæ*, wild-ducks, and some others, are very long, and give their wings, when the motion, an hooked appearance. Dab-chicks, moor-hens, and coots, fly erect, with their legs hanging down, and hardly make any dispatch; the reason is plain, their wings are placed too forward out of the true centre of gravity; as the legs of auks and divers are situated too backward.

*   *   *

From the motion of birds, the transition is natural enough to their notes and language, of which I shall say something. Not that I would pretend to understand their language like the vizer who, by the recital of a conversation which passed between two owls, reclaimed a sultan, before delighting in conquest and devastation; but I would be thought only to mean that many of the winged tribes have various sounds and voices adapted to express their various passions, wants, and feelings; such as anger, fear, love, hatred, hunger and the like. All species are not equally eloquent; some are copious and fluent as it were in their utterance, while others are confined to a few important sounds: no bird, like the fish kind, is quite mute, though some are rather silent. The language of birds is very ancient, and, like other ancient modes of speech, very elliptical: little is said, but much is meant and understood.

The notes of the eagle-kind are shrill and piercing; and about the season of nidification much diversified, as I have been often assured by a curious observer of nature, who long resided at Gibraltar, where eagles abound. The notes of our hawks much resemble those of the king of birds. Owls have very expressive notes; they hoot in a fine vocal sound, much resembling the *vox humana*, and reducible by a pitch-pipe to a musical key. This note seems to express complacency and rivalry among the males; they use also a quick call and an horrible scream; and can snore and hiss when they mean to menace. Ravens, beside their loud croak, can exert a deep and solemn note that makes the woods to echo; the amorous sound of a crow is strange and ridiculous; rooks, in the breeding season, attempt sometimes in the gaiety of their hearts to sing, but with no great success; the parrot-kind have many modulations of voice, as appears by their aptitude to learn human sounds; doves coo in an amorous and mournful manner, and are emblems of despairing lovers; the wood-pecker sets up a sort of loud and hearty laugh; the fern-owl, or goat-sucker, from the dusk till day-break, serenades his mate with the clattering of castanets. All the tuneful *passeres* express their complacency by sweet modulations, and a variety of melody. The swallow, as has been observed in a former letter, by a shrill alarm bespeaks the attention of the other *hirundines*, and bids them be aware that the hawk is at hand. Aquatic and gregarious birds, especially the nocturnal, that shift their quarters in the dark, are very noisy and loquacious; as cranes, wild-geese, wild-ducks, and the like; their perpetual clamour prevents them from dispersing and losing their companions.

In so extensive a subject, sketches and outlines are as much as can be expected; for it would be endless to instance in all the infinite variety of the feathered nation. We shall therefore confine the remainder of this letter to the few domestic fowls of our yards, which are most known, and therefore best understood. At first the peacock, with his gorgeous train, demands our attention; but, like most of the gaudy birds, his notes are grating and shocking to the ear: the yelling of cats, and the braying of an ass, are not more disgustful. The voice of the goose is trumpet-like, and clanking; and once saved the Capitol at Rome, as grave historians assert: the hiss also of the gander is formidable and full of menace, and 'protective of his young.' Among ducks the sexual distinction of voice is remarkable; for, while the quack of the female is loud and sonorous, the voice of the drake is inward and harsh and feeble, and scarce discernible. The cock turkey struts and gobbles to his mistress in a most uncouth manner; he hath also a pert and petulant note when he attacks his adversary. When a hen turkey leads forth her young brood she keeps a watchful eye:

and if a bird of prey appear, though ever so high in the air, the careful mother announces the enemy with a little inward moan, and watches him with a steady and attentive look; but if he approach, her note becomes earnest and alarming, and her outcries are redoubled.

No inhabitants of a yard seem possessed of such a variety of expression and so copious a language as common poultry. Take a chicken of four or five days old, and hold it up to a window where there are flies, and it will immediately seize its prey, with little twitterings of complacency; but if you tender it a wasp or a bee, at once its note becomes harsh, and expressive of disapprobation and a sense of danger. When a pullet is ready to lay she intimates the event by a joyous and easy soft note. Of all the occurrences of their life that of laying seems to be the most important; for no sooner has a hen disburdened herself, than she rushes forth with a clamorous kind of joy, which the cock and the rest of his mistresses immediately adopt. The tumult is not confined to the family concerned, but catches from yard to yard, and spreads to every homestead within hearing, till at last the whole village is in an uproar. As soon as a hen becomes a mother her new relation demands a new language; she then runs clocking and screaming about, and seems agitated as if possessed. The father of the flock has also a considerable vocabulary; if he finds food, he calls a favourite concubine to partake; and if a bird of prey passes over, with a warning voice he bids his family beware. The gallant chanticleer has, at command, his amorous phrases, and his terms of defiance. But the sound by which he is best known is his crowing: by this he has been distinguished in all ages as the countryman's clock or larum, as the watchman that proclaims the divisions of the night. Thus the poet elegantly styles him:

> . . . the crested cock, whose clarion sounds
> The silent hours.

A neighbouring gentleman one summer had lost most of his chickens by a sparrow-hawk, that came gliding down between a faggot-pile and the end of his house to the place where the coops stood. The owner, inwardly vexed to see his flock thus diminishing, hung a setting net adroitly between the pile and the house, into which the caitiff dashed and was entangled. Resentment suggested the law of retaliation: he therefore clipped the hawk's wings, cut off his talons, and, fixing a cork on his bill, threw him down among the brood-hens. Imagination cannot paint the scene that ensued; the expressions that fear, rage, and revenge inspired, were new, or at least such as had been unnoticed before: the exasperated matrons upbraided, they execrated, they insulted, they triumphed. In a word, they never desisted from buffeting their adversary till they had torn him in an hundred pieces.

*   *   *

It is now more than forty years that I have paid some attention to the ornithology of this district, without being able to exhaust the subject: new occurrences still arise as long as any inquiries are kept alive.

In the last week of last month five of those most rare birds, too uncommon to have obtained an English name, but known to naturalists by the terms of *himantopus*, or *loripes*, and *charadrius himantopus*, were shot upon the verge of Frinsham-pond, a large lake belonging to the bishop of Winchester, and lying between Wolmer-forest, and the town of Farnham, in the county of Surrey. The pond keeper says there were three brace in the flock; but that, after he had satisfied his curiosity, he suffered the sixth to remain unmolested. One of these specimens I procured, and found the length of the legs to be so extraordinary, that, at first sight, one might have supposed the shanks had been fastened on to impose on the credulity of the beholder: they were legs in *caricatura*; and had we seen such proportions on a Chinese or Japan screen we should have made large allowances for the fancy of the draughtsman. These birds are of the plover family, and might with propriety be called the stilt plovers. Brisson, under that idea, gives them the apposite name of *l'échasse*. My specimen, when drawn and stuffed with pepper, weighed only four ounces and a quarter, though the naked part of the thigh measured three inches and an half, and the legs four inches and an half. Hence we may safely assert that these birds exhibit, weight for inches, incomparably the greatest length of legs of any known bird. The flamingo, for instance, is one of the most long legged birds, and yet it bears no manner of proportion to the *himantopus*; for a cock flamingo weighs, at an average, about four pounds avoirdupois; and his legs and thighs measure usually about twenty inches. But four pounds are fifteen times and a fraction more than four ounces and one quarter; and if four ounces and a quarter have eight inches of legs, four pounds must have one hundred and twenty inches and a fraction of legs; viz., somewhat more than ten feet; such a monstrous proportion as the world never saw! If you should try the experiment in still larger birds the disparity would still increase. It must be matter of great curiosity to see the stilt plover move; to observe how it can wield such a length of lever with such feeble muscles as the thighs seem to be furnished with. At best one should expect it to be but a bad walker: but what adds to the wonder is that it has no back toe. Now without that steady prop to support its steps it must be liable, in speculation, to perpetual vacillations, and seldom able to preserve the true centre of gravity.

The old name of *himantopus* is taken from Pliny; and, by an awkward metaphor, implies that the legs are as slender and pliant as if cut out of a thong of leather. Neither Willughby nor Ray, in all their curious researches either at home or abroad, ever saw this bird. Mr Pennant never met with it in all Great Britain, but observed it often in the cabinets of the curious at Paris. Hasselquist says that it migrates to Egypt in the autumn: and a most accurate observer of nature has assured me that he has found it on the banks of the streams in Andalusia.

Our writers record it to have been found only twice in Great Britain. From all these relations it plainly appears that these long-legged plovers are birds of South Europe, and rarely visit our island; and when they do are wanderers and stragglers, and impelled to make so distant and northern an excursion from motives or accidents for which we are not able to account. One thing may fairly be deduced, that these birds come over to us from the continent, since nobody can suppose that a species not noticed once in an age, and of such a remarkable make, can constantly breed unobserved in this kingdom.

THE STORY OF PENGUIN CLASSICS

Before 1946 ...'Classics' are mainly the domain of academics and students, without readable editions for everyone else. This all changes when a little-known classicist, E. V. Rieu, presents Penguin founder Allen Lane with the translation of Homer's Odyssey that he has been working on and reading to his wife Nelly in his spare time.

1946 The Odyssey becomes the first Penguin Classic published, and promptly sells three million copies. Suddenly, classic books are no longer for the privileged few.

1950s Rieu, now series editor, turns to professional writers for the best modern, readable translations, including Dorothy L. Sayers's *Inferno* and Robert Graves's *The Twelve Caesars*, which revives the salacious original.

1960s 1961 sees the arrival of the Penguin Modern Classics, showcasing the best twentieth-century writers from around the world. Rieu retires in 1964, hailing the Penguin Classics list as 'the greatest educative force of the 20th century'.

1970s A new generation of translators arrives to swell the Penguin Classics ranks, and the list grows to encompass more philosophy, religion, science, history and politics.

1980s The Penguin American Library joins the Classics stable, with titles such as *The Last of the Mohicans* safeguarded. Penguin Classics now offers the most comprehensive library of world literature available.

1990s Penguin Popular Classics are launched, offering readers budget editions of the greatest works of literature. Penguin Audiobooks brings the classics to a listening audience for the first time, and in 1999 the launch of the Penguin Classics website takes them online to an ever larger global readership.

The 21st Century Penguin Classics are rejacketed for the first time in nearly twenty years. This world famous series now consists of more than 1,300 titles, making the widest range of the best books ever written available to millions – and constantly redefining the meaning of what makes a 'classic'.

The Odyssey continues ...

The best books ever written

PENGUIN 🐧 CLASSICS

SINCE 1946